The Amazing Mandala Coloring Book #1

Marie Smith

I0493714

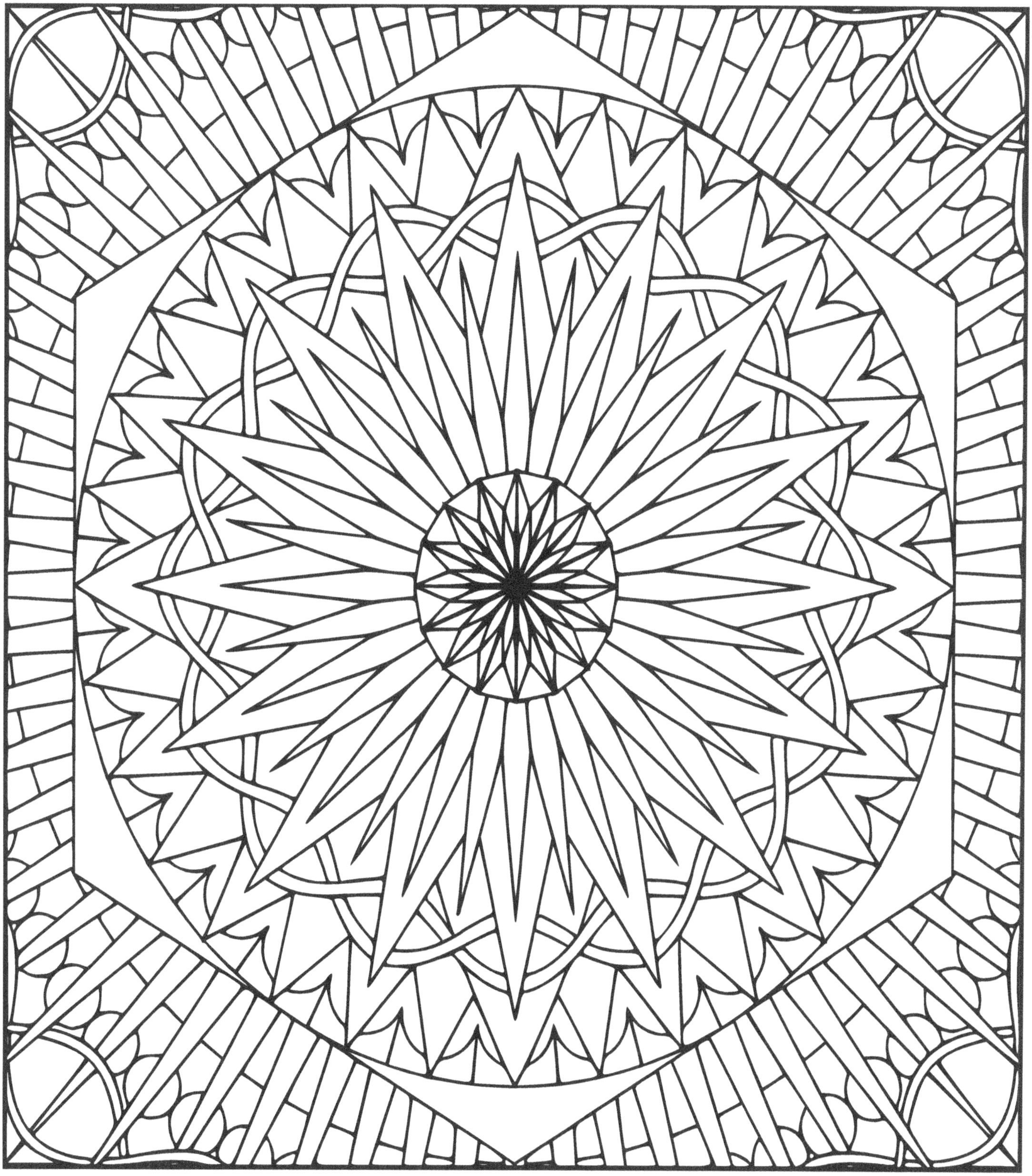

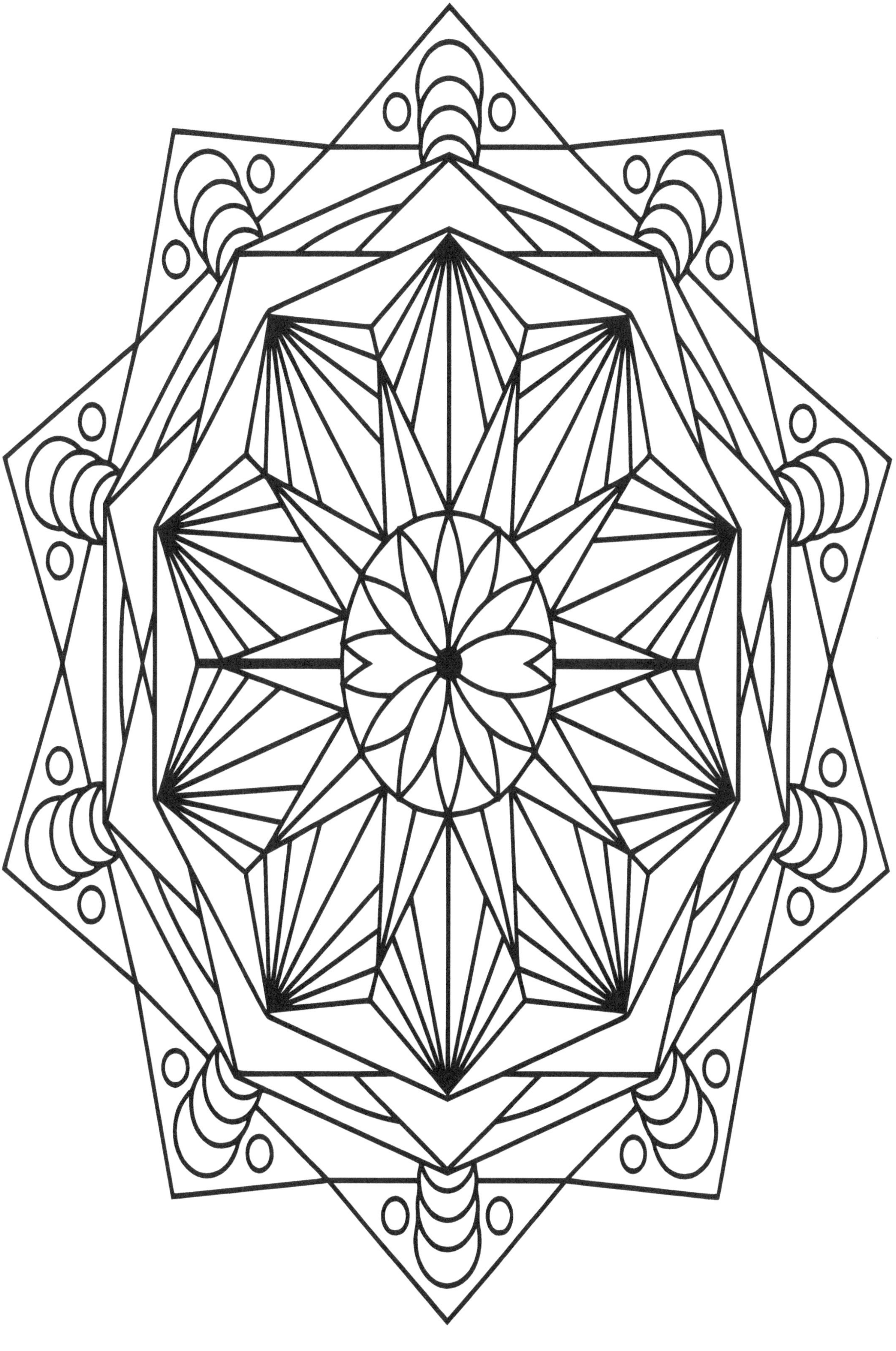

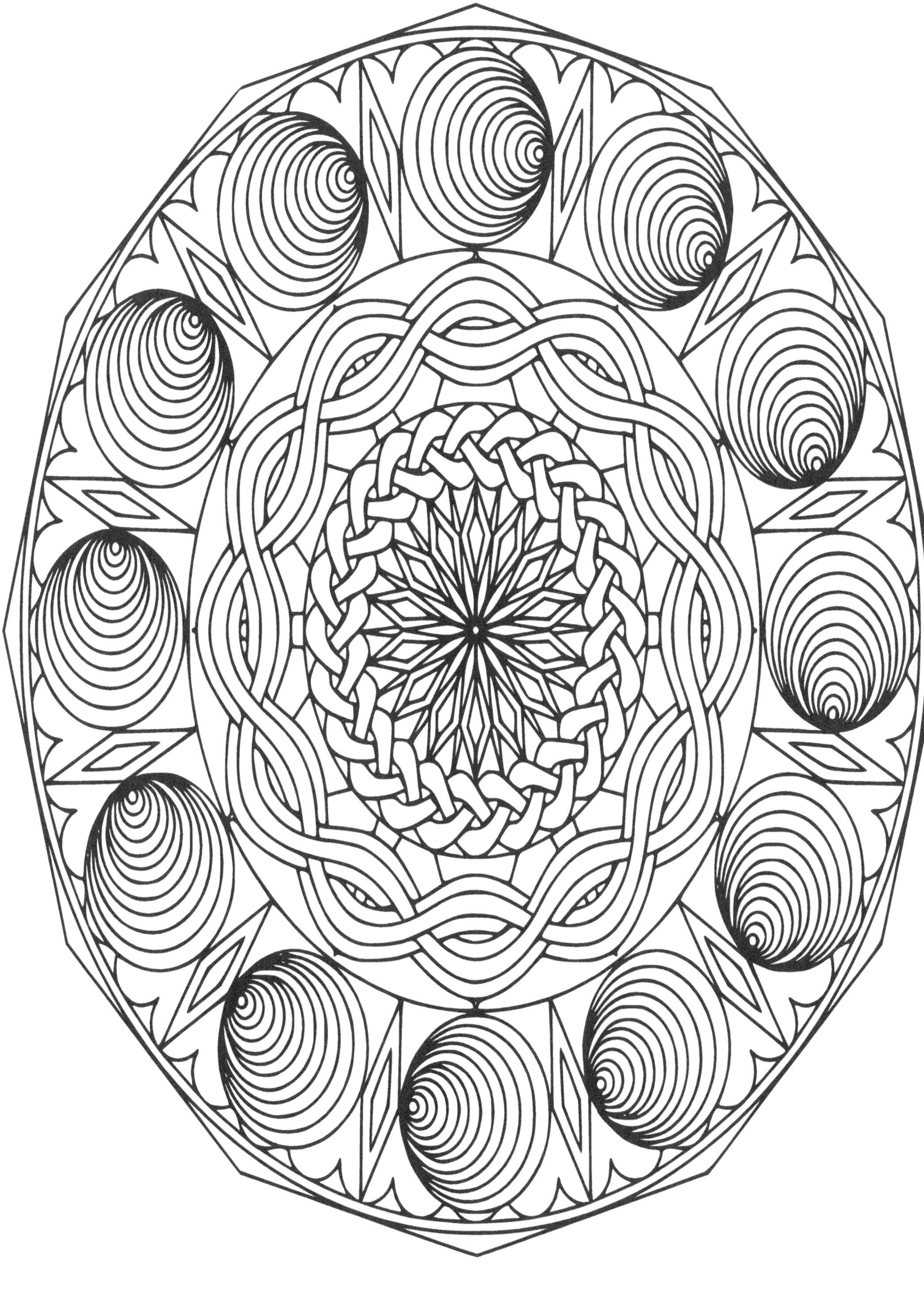

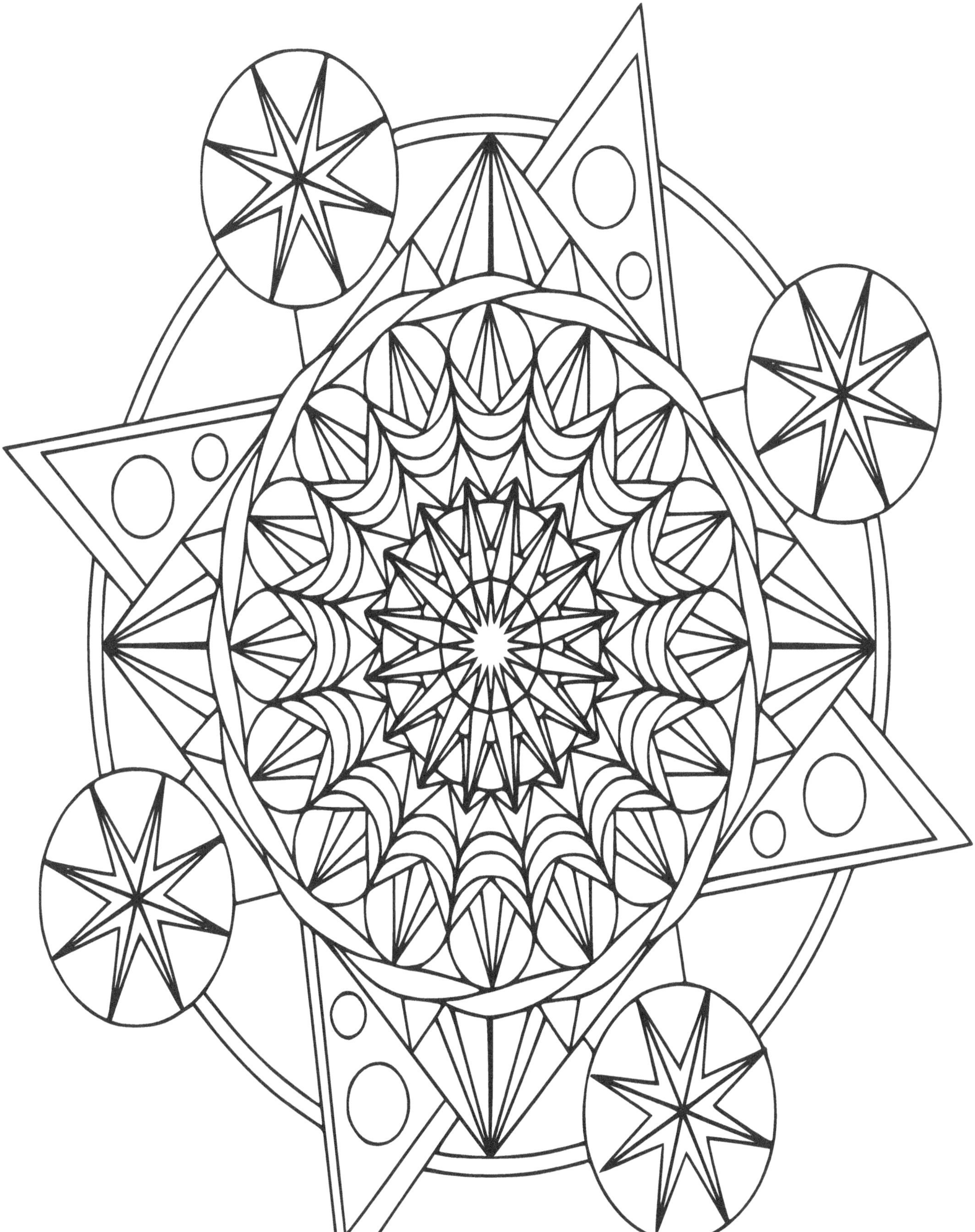

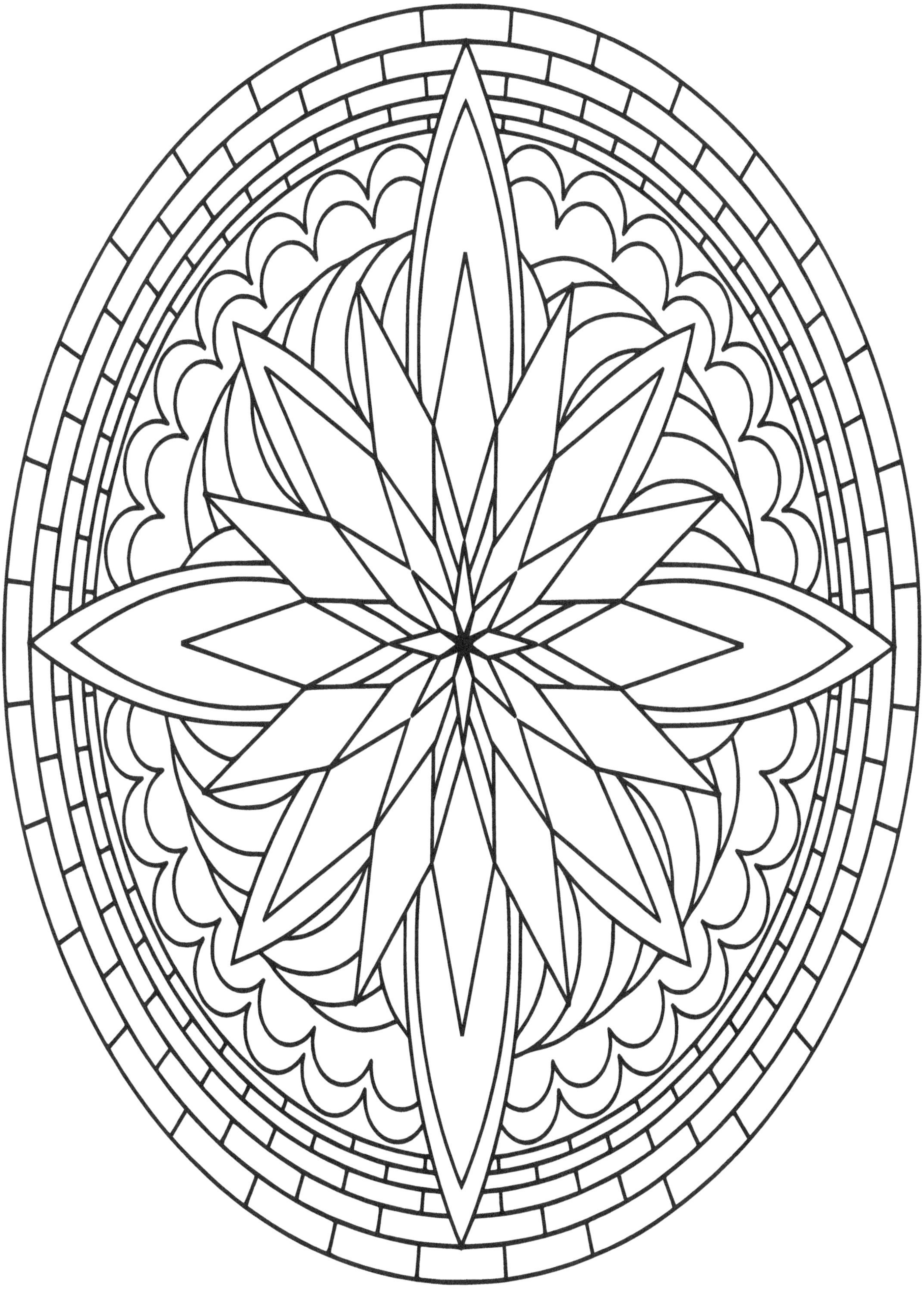

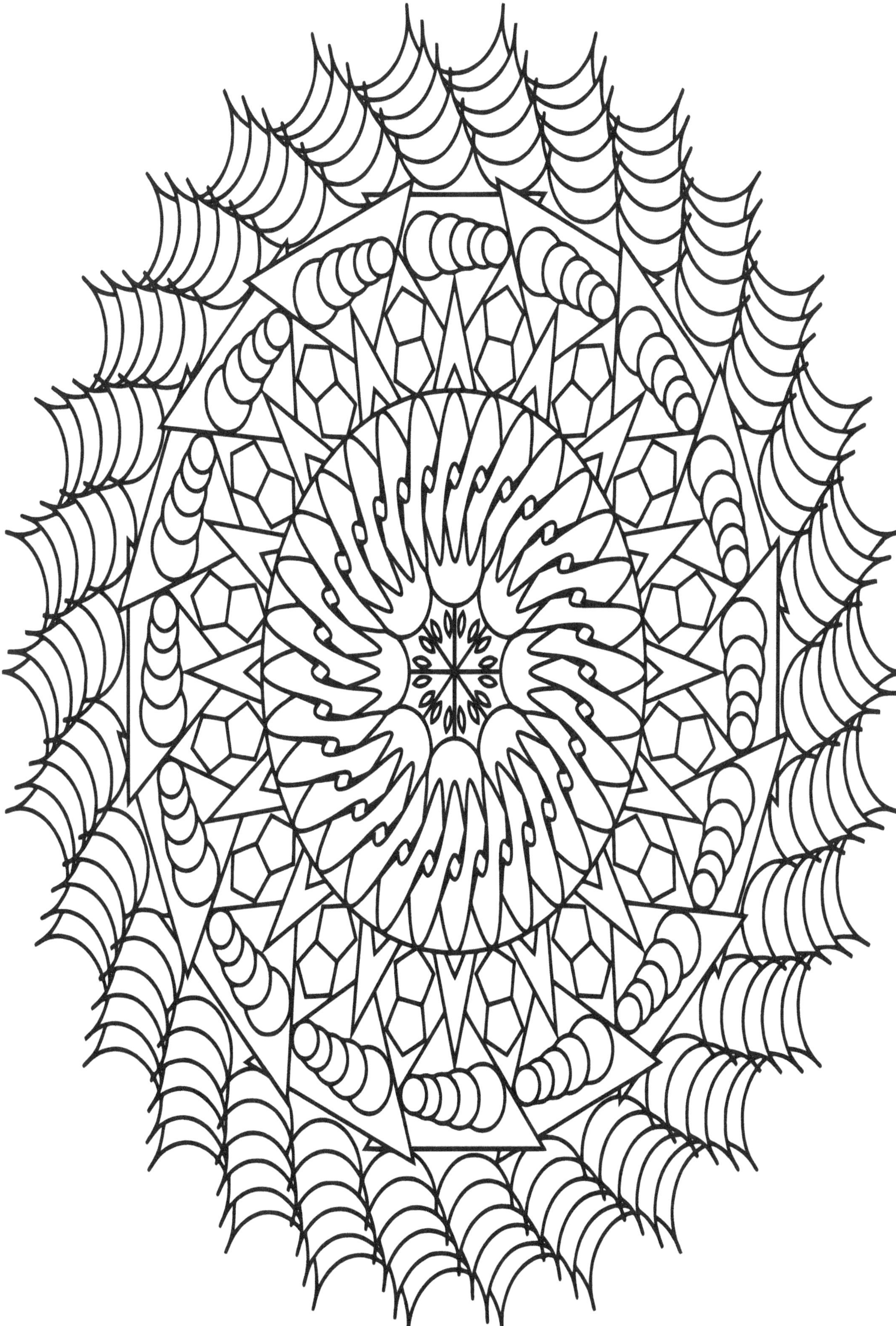

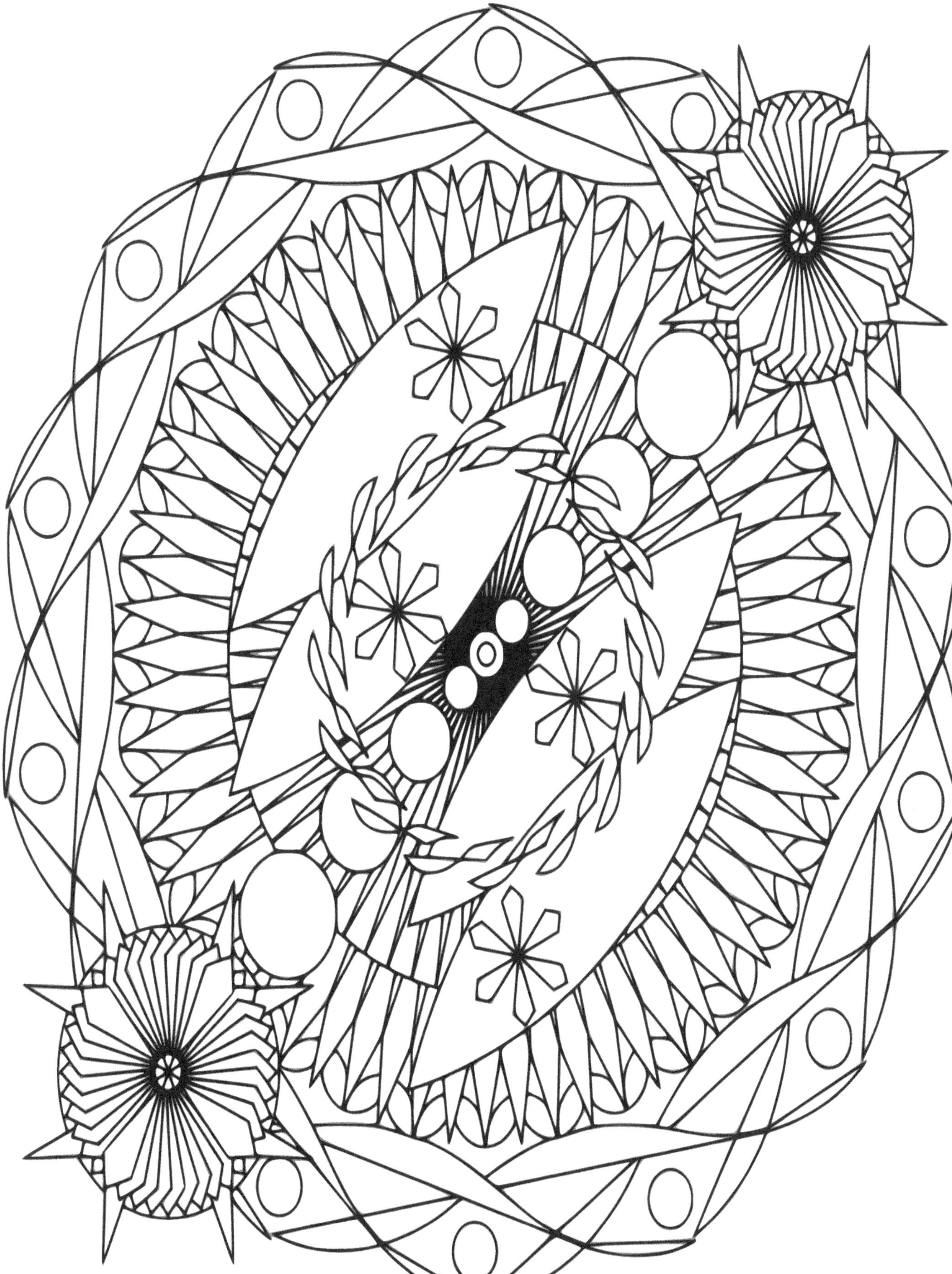

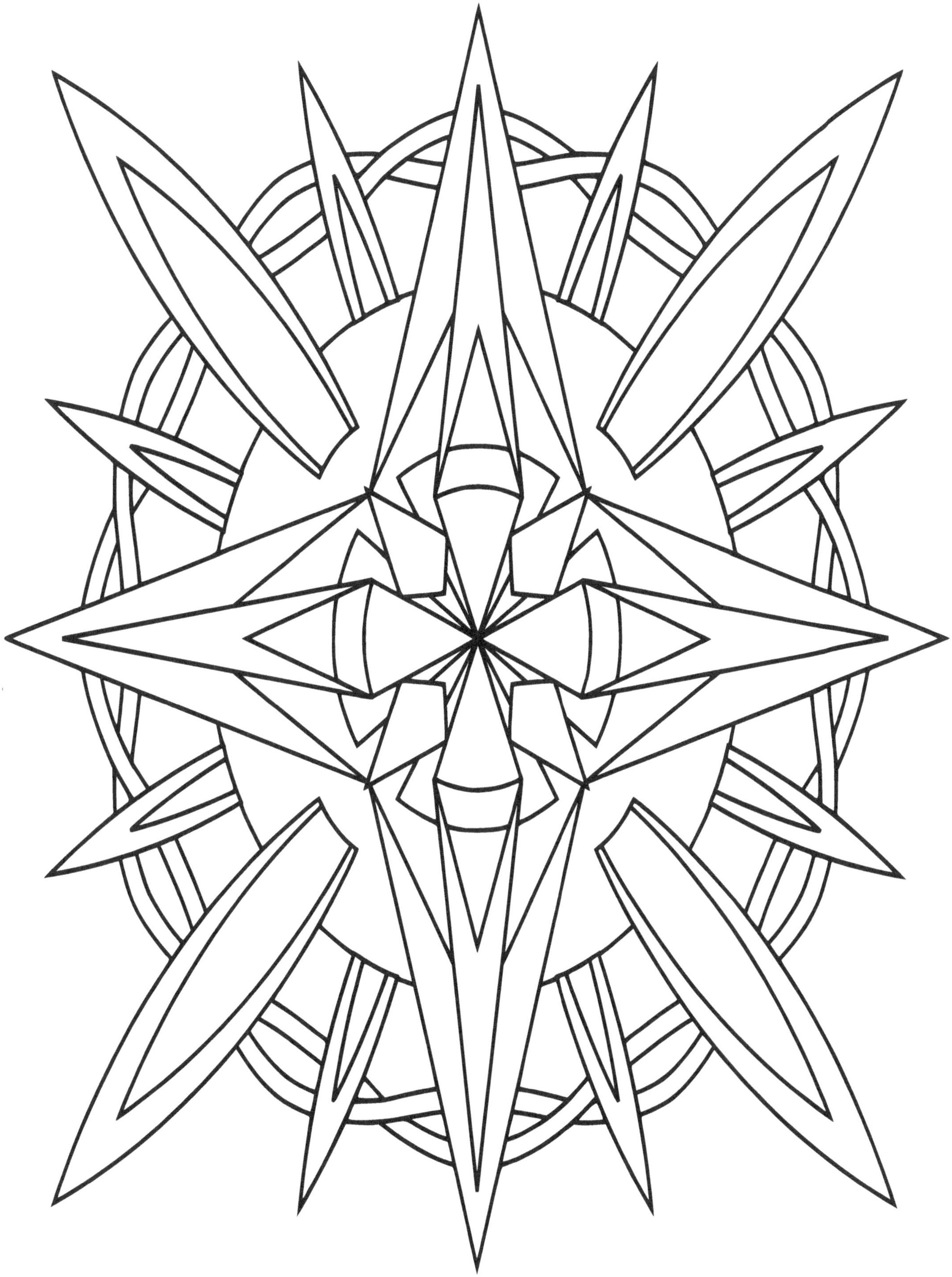

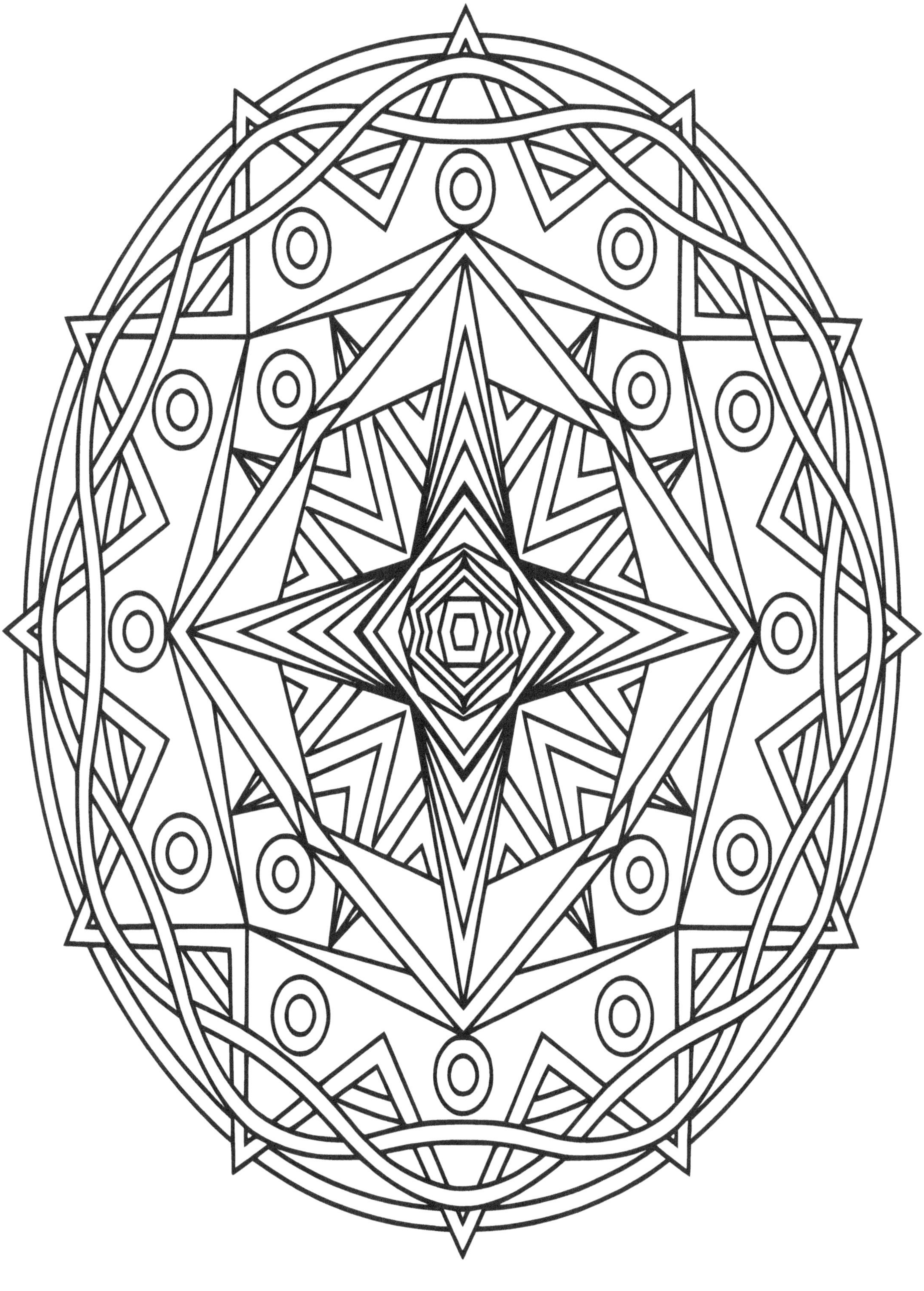

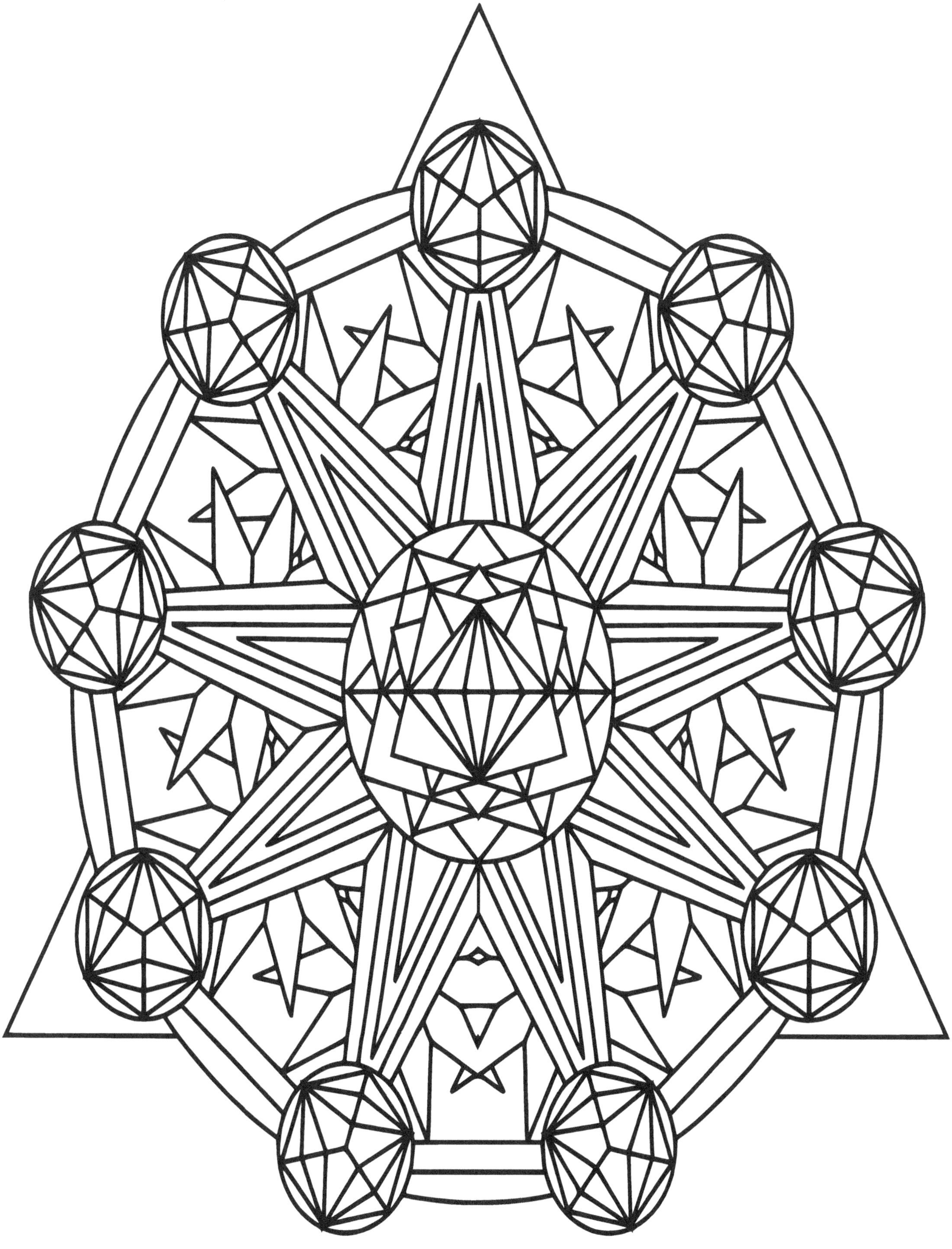

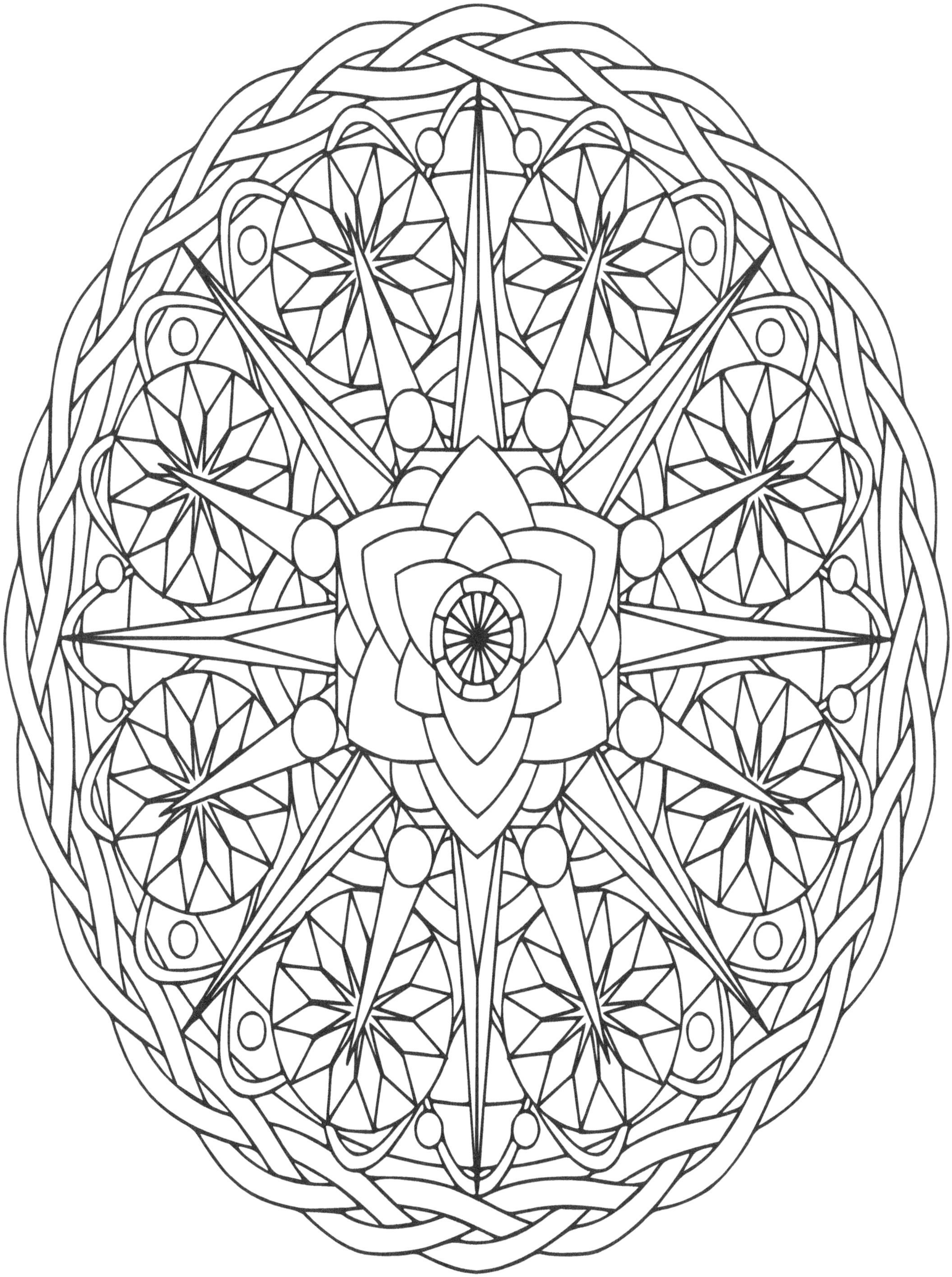

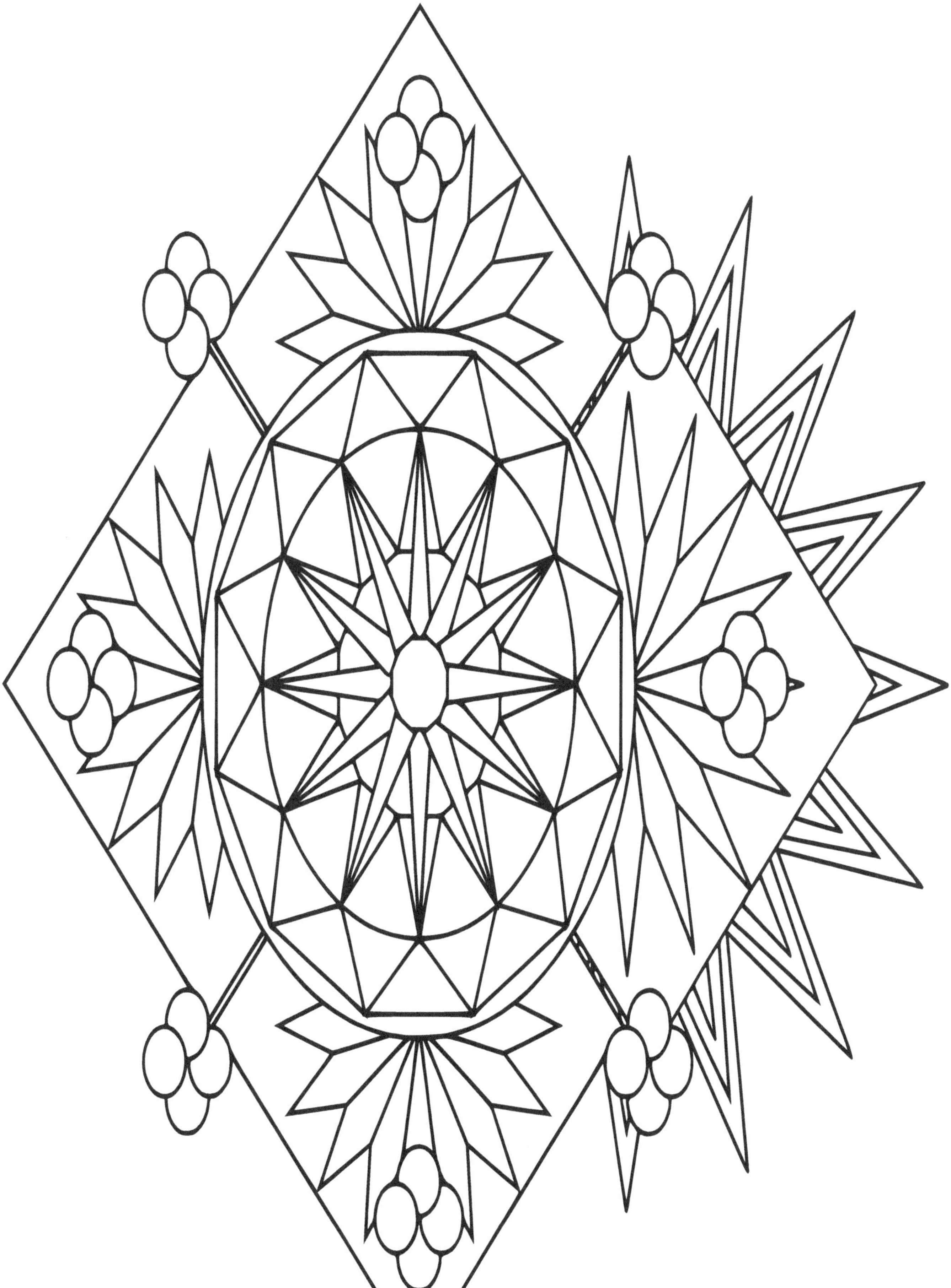

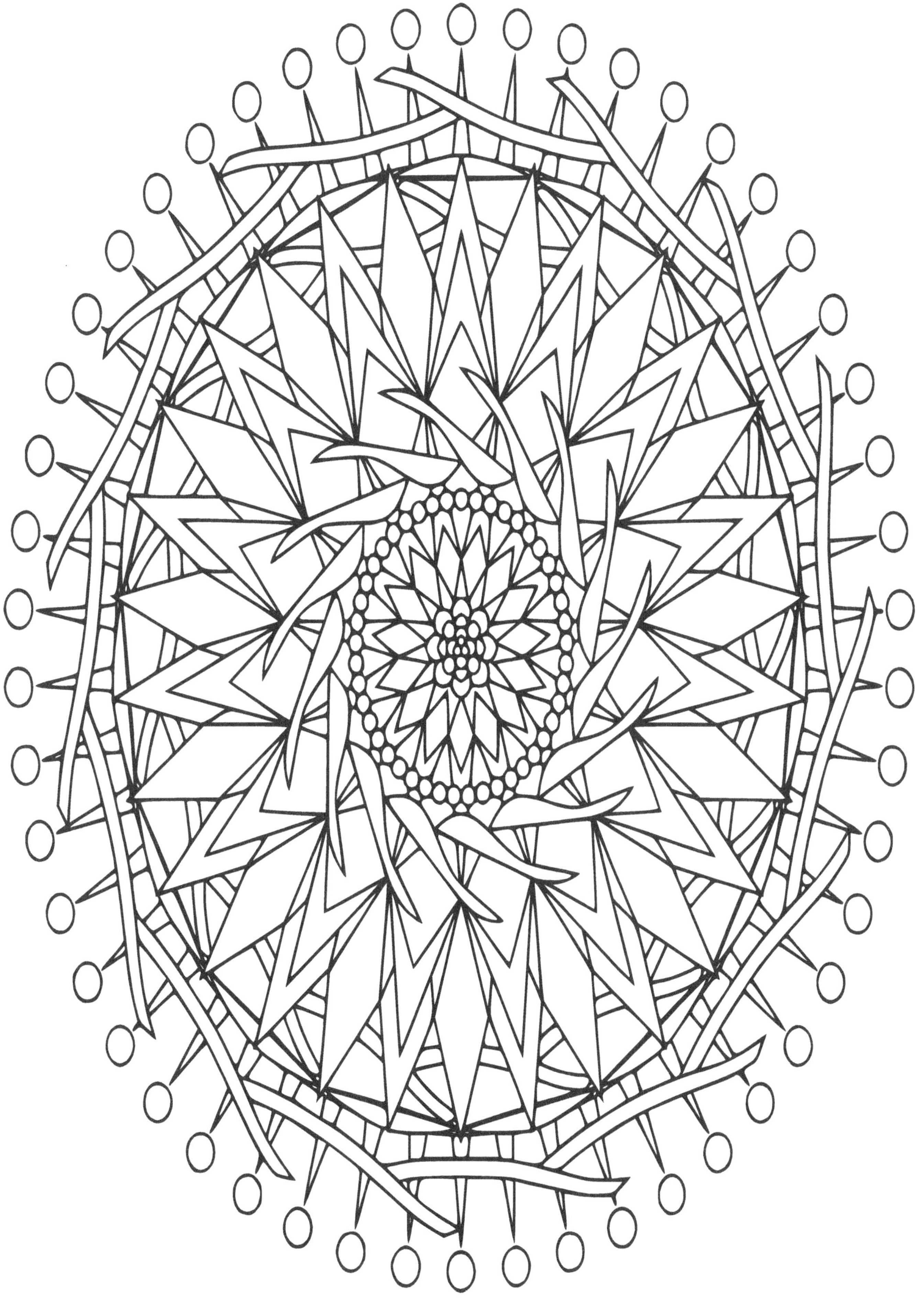

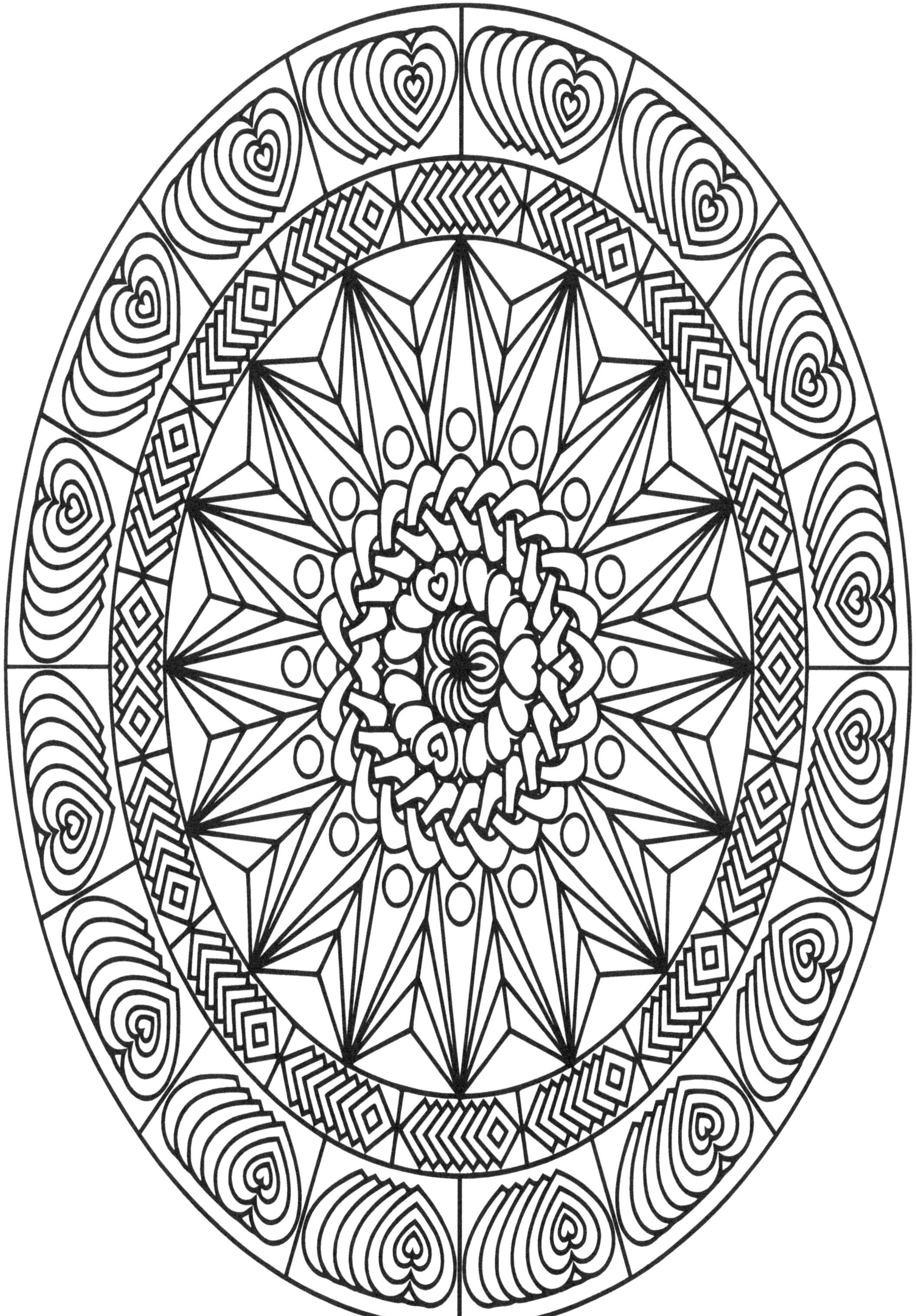

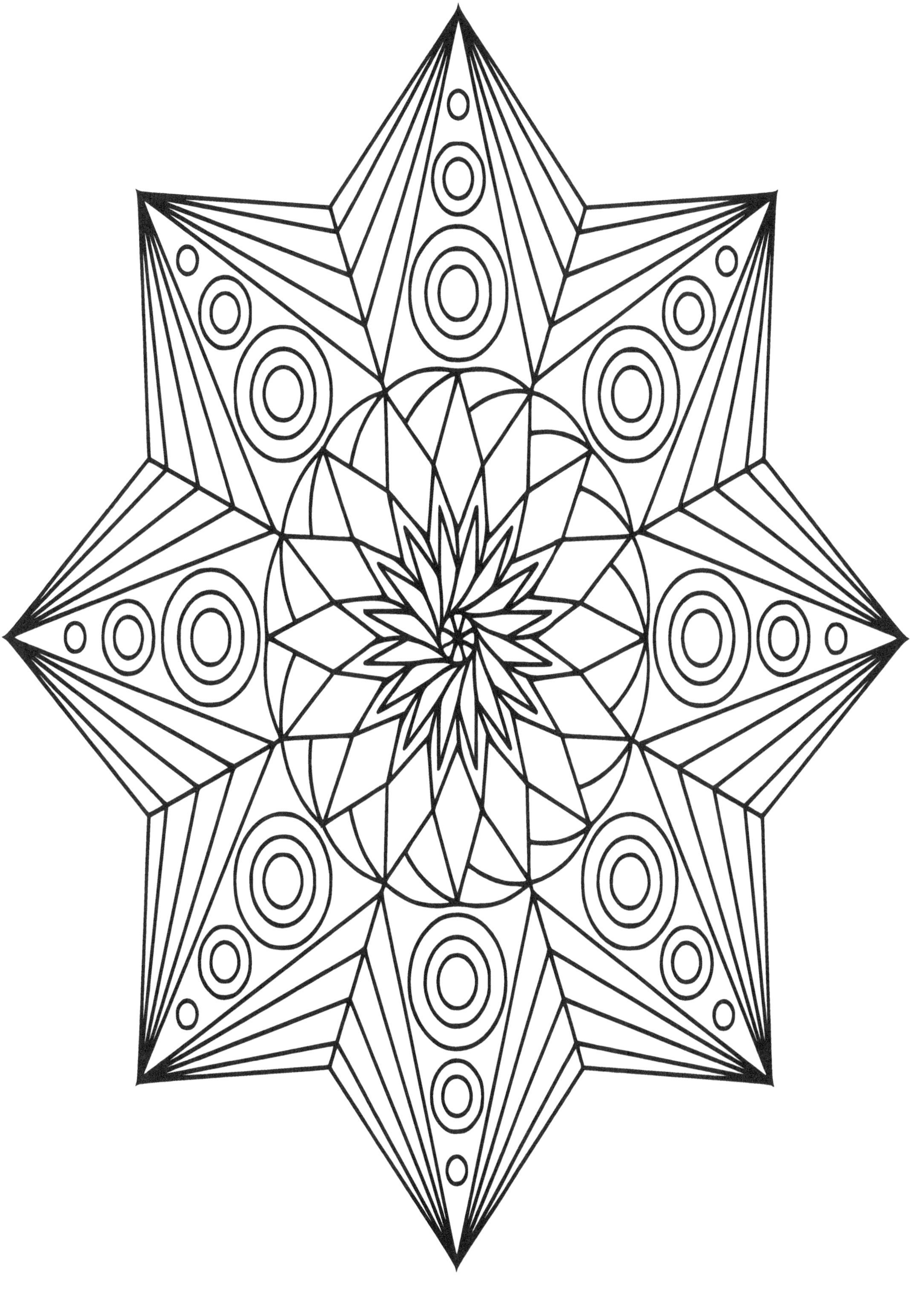

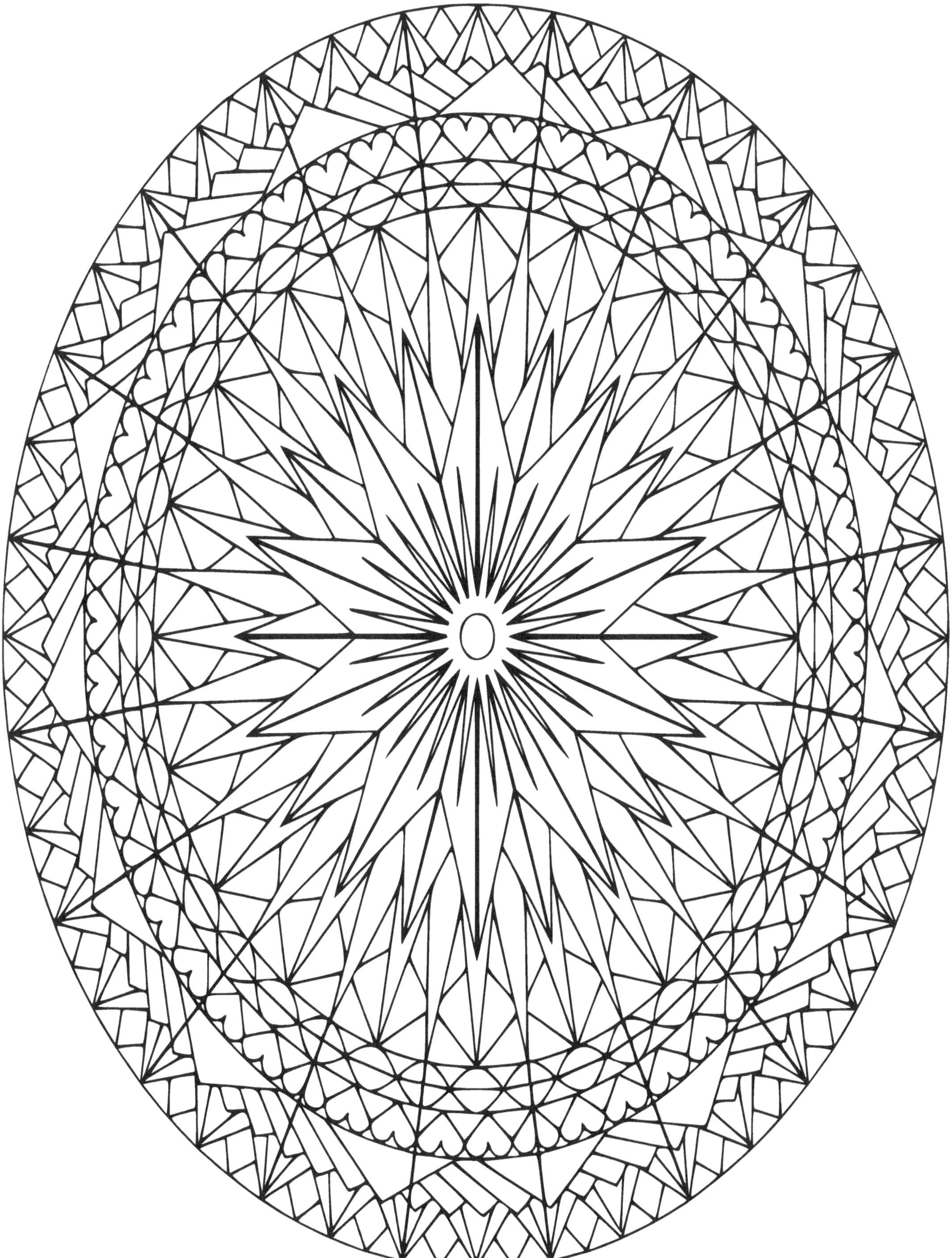

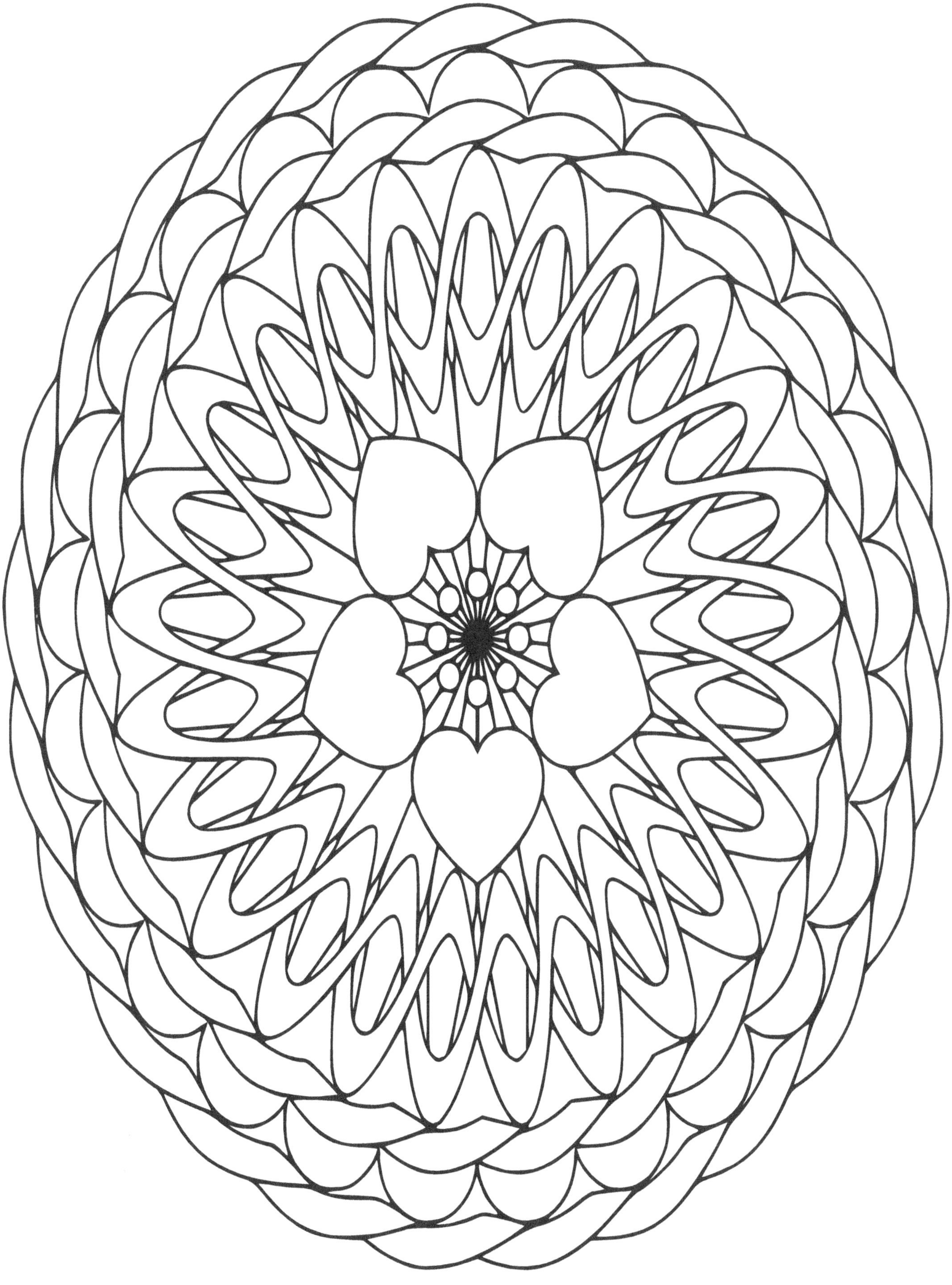

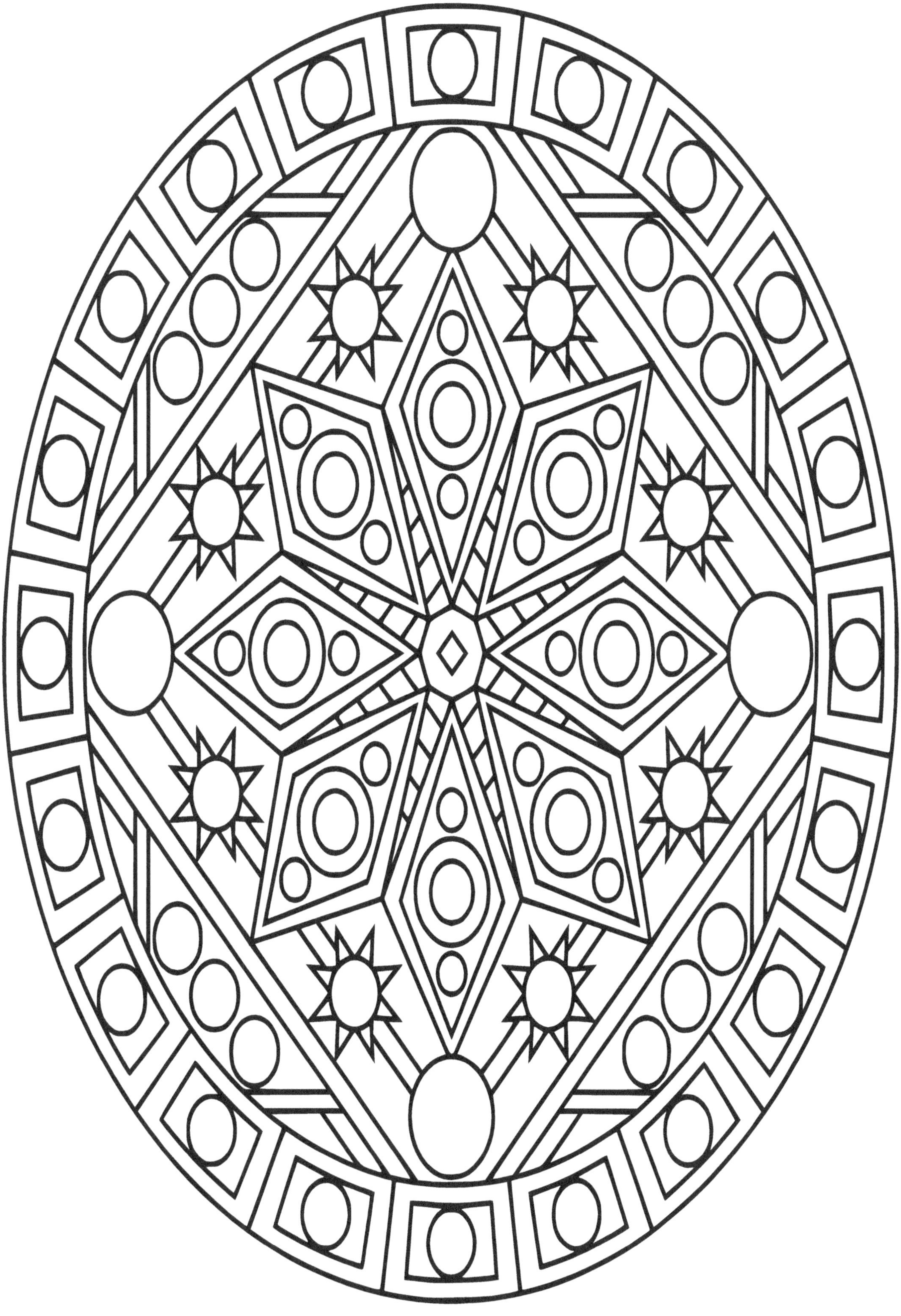

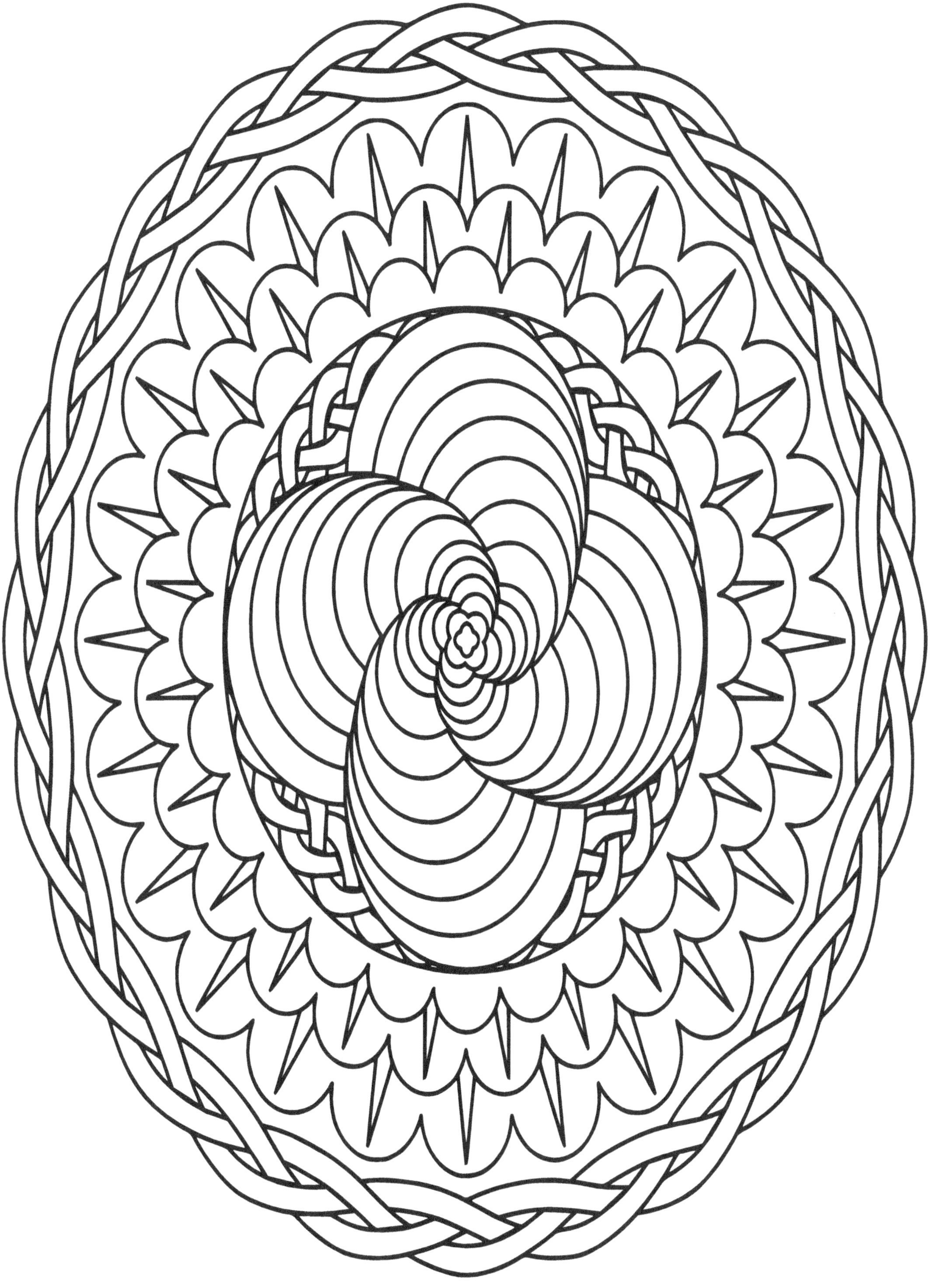

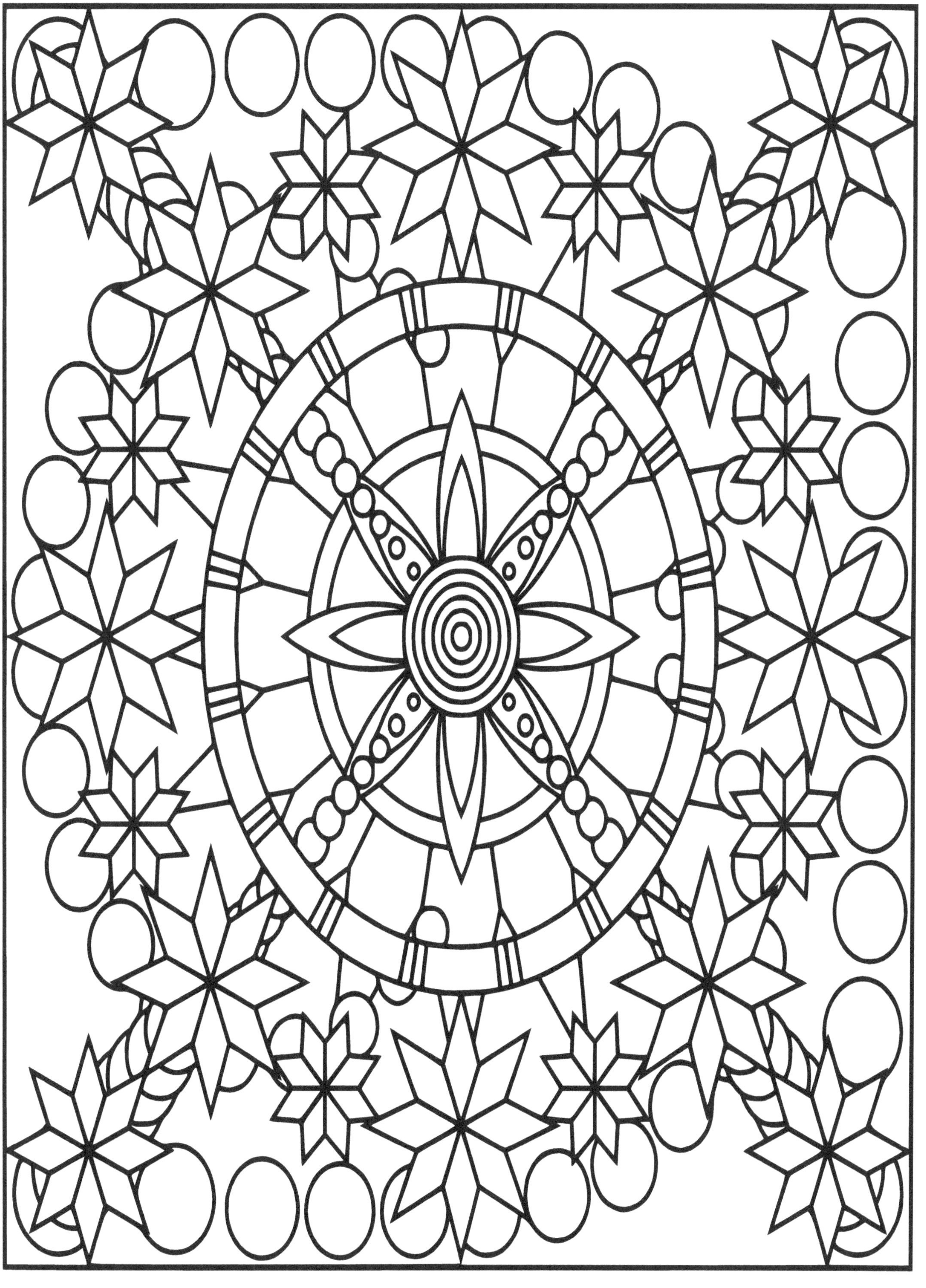

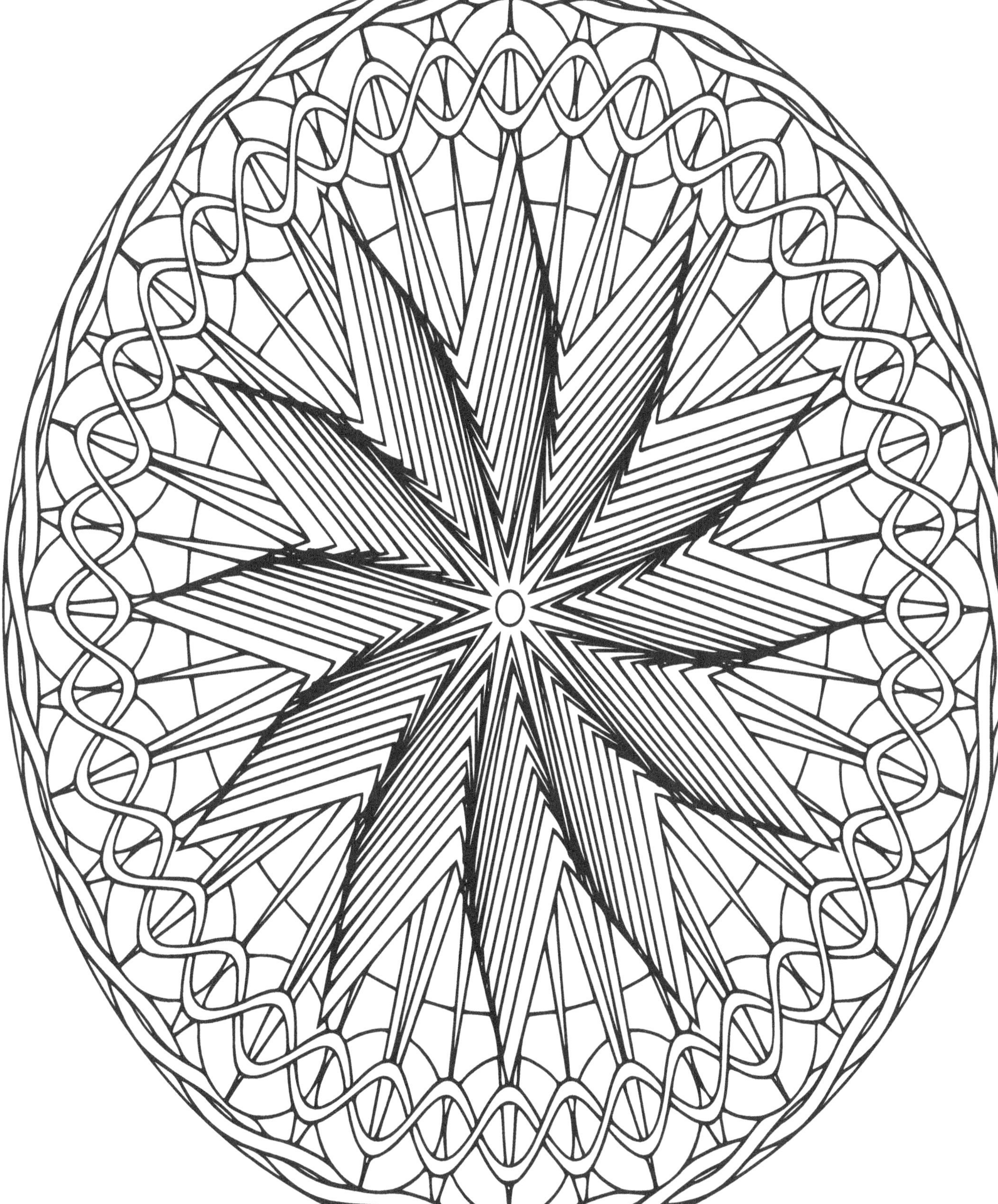

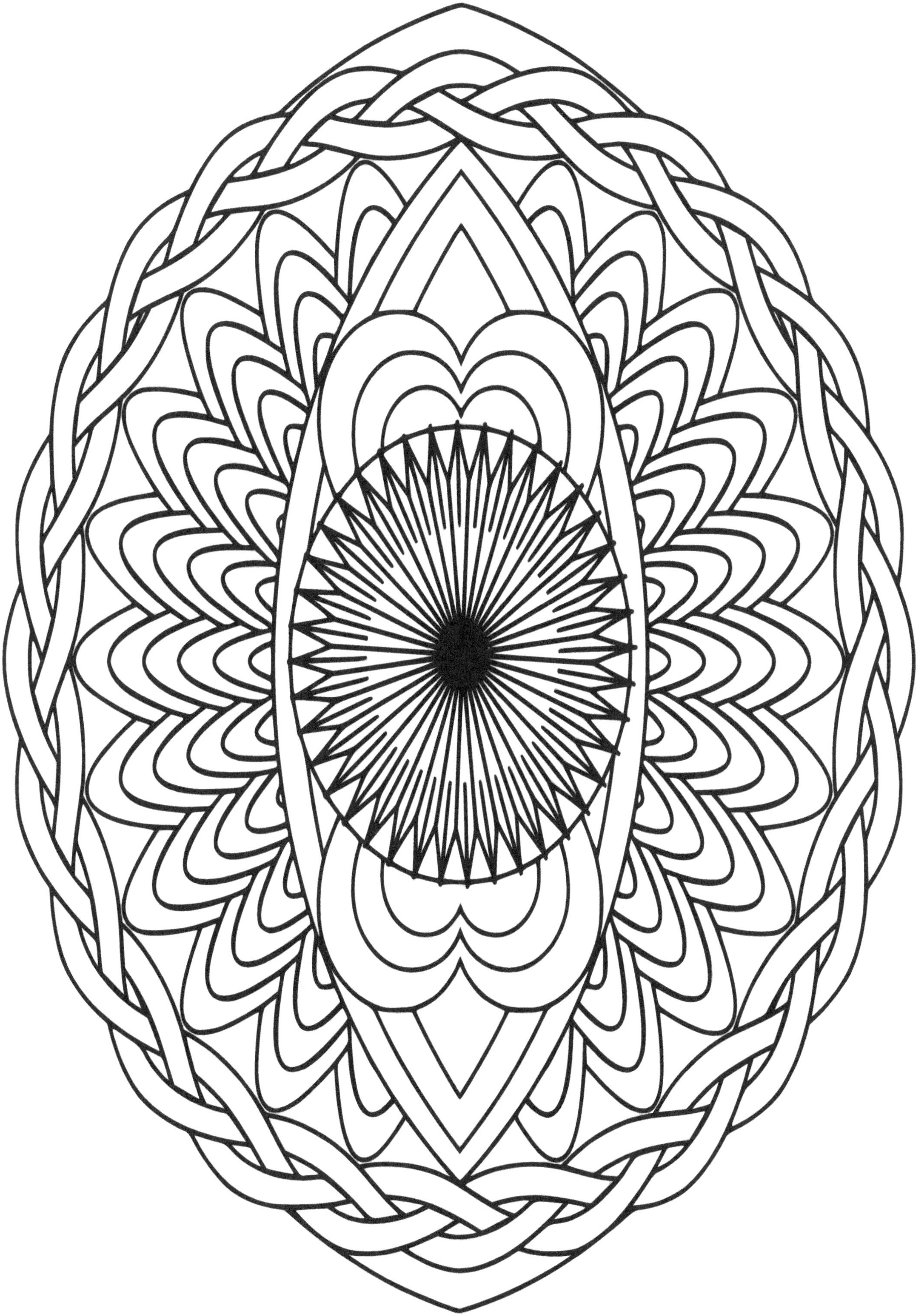

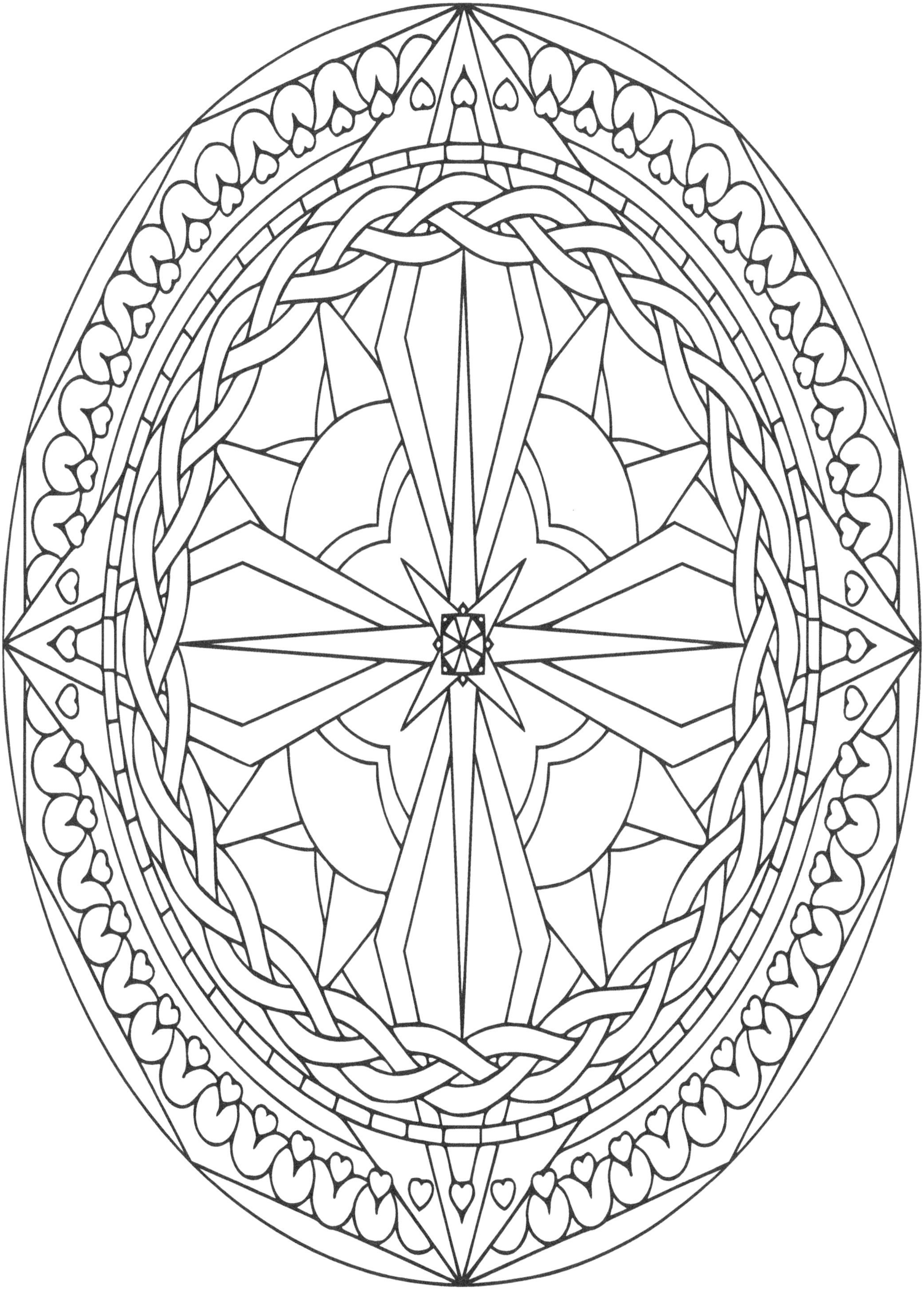

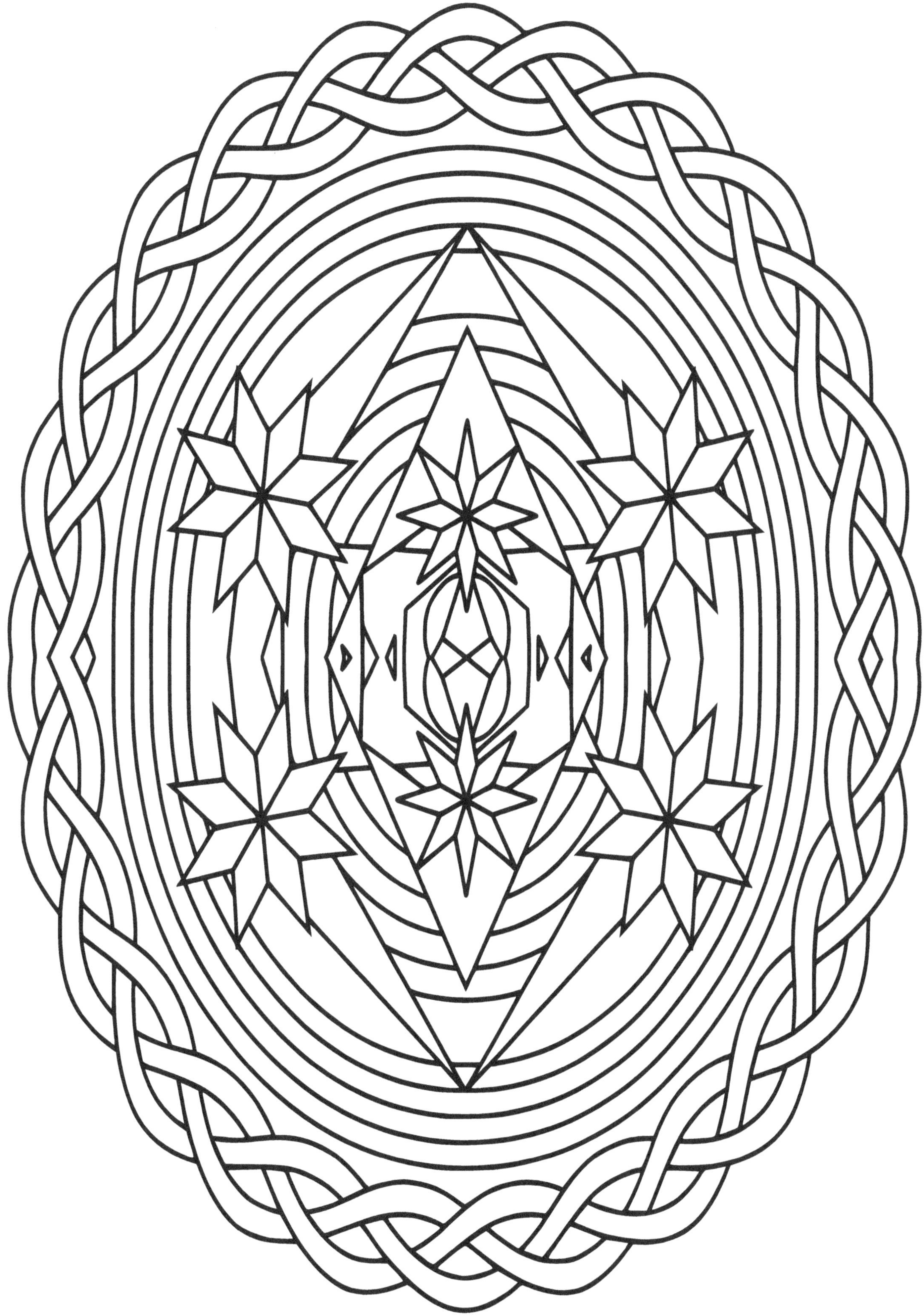

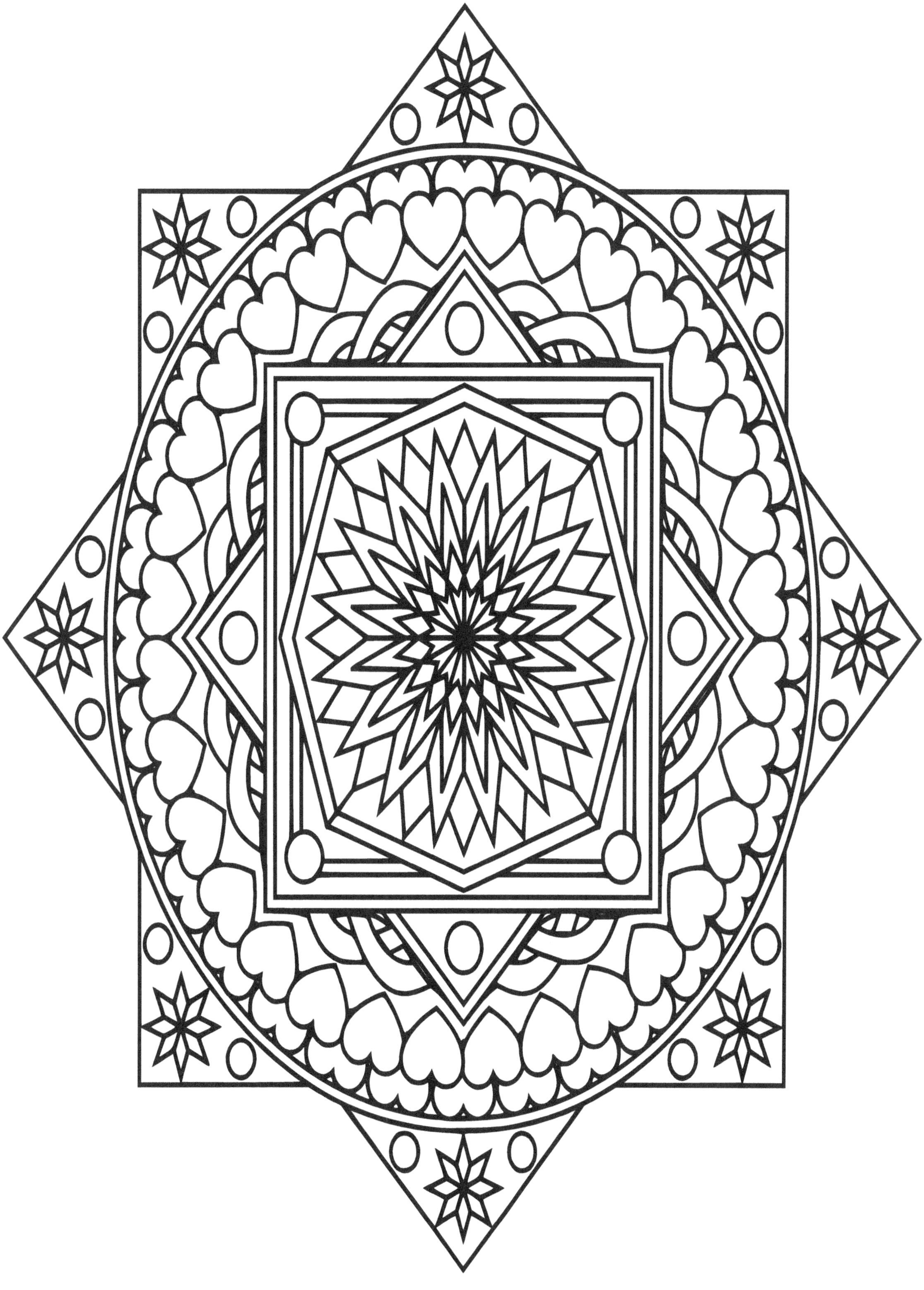

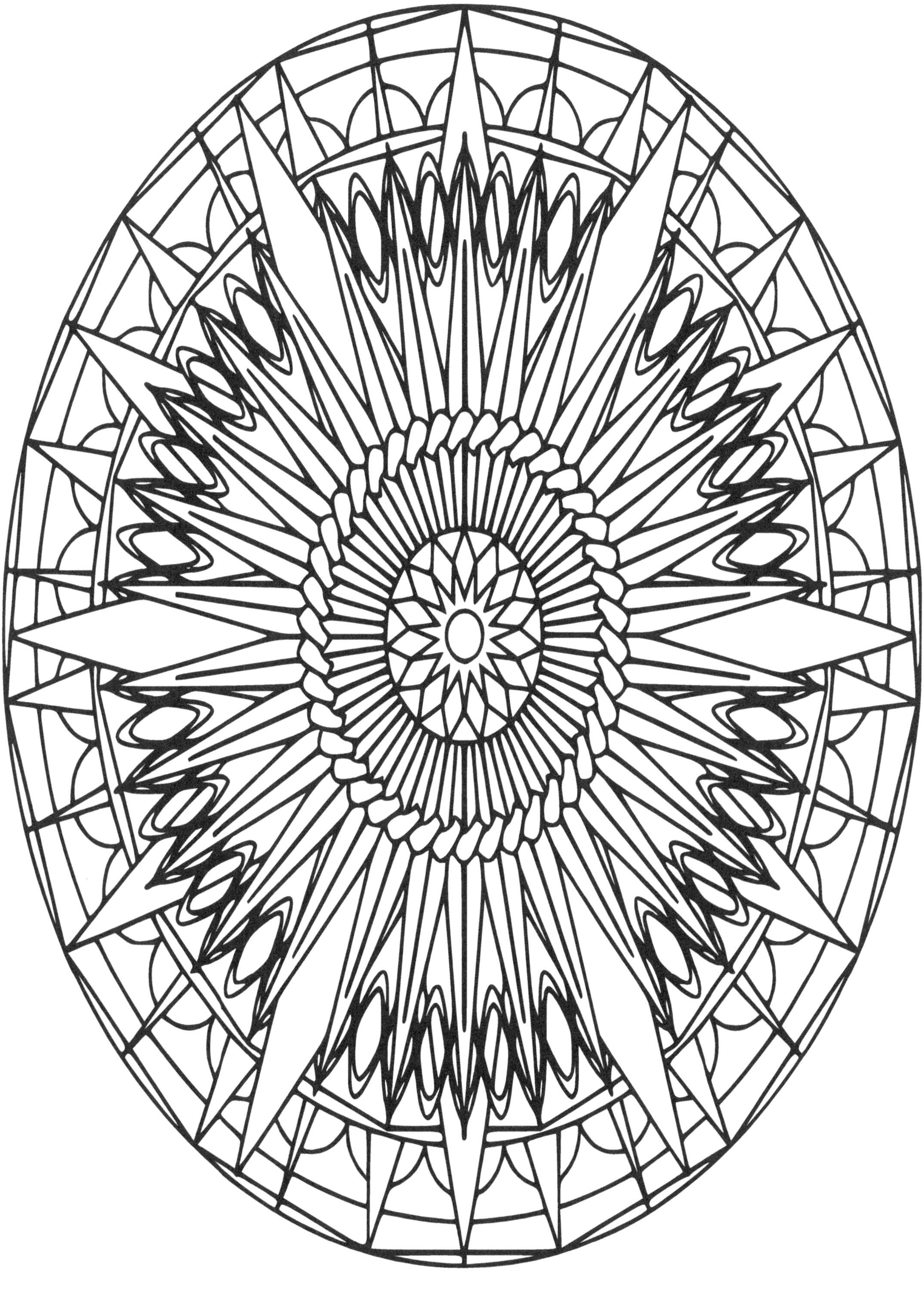

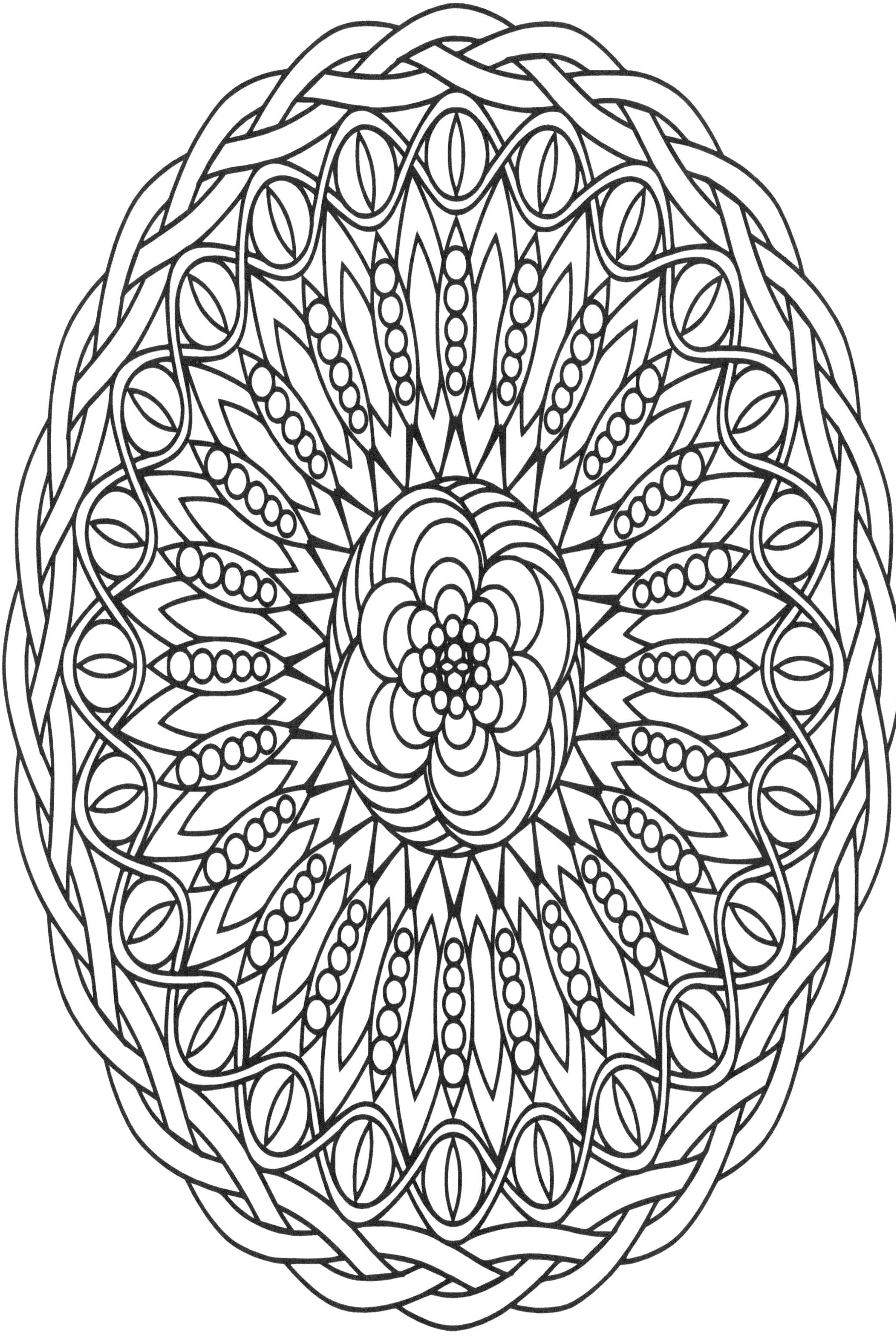

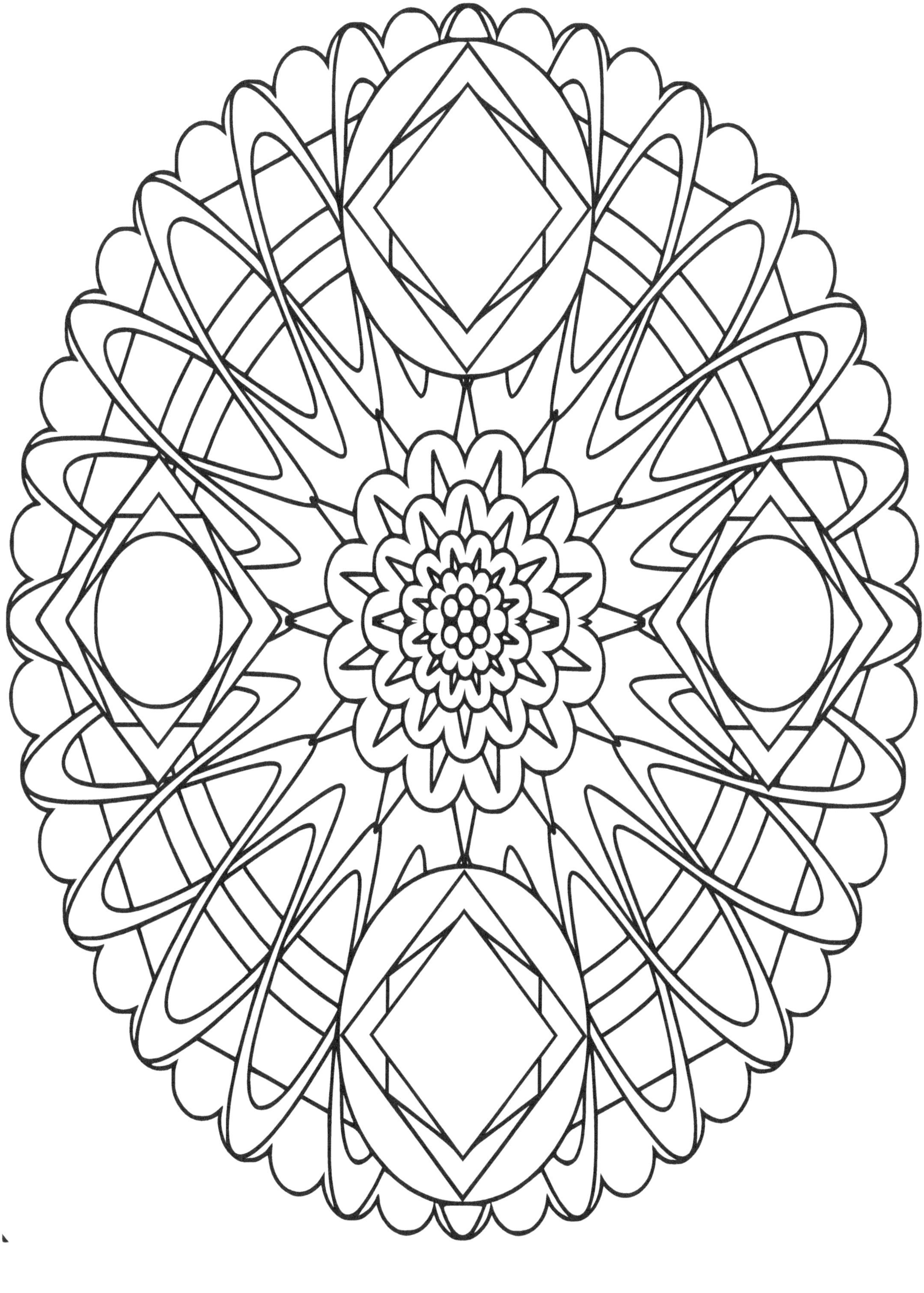

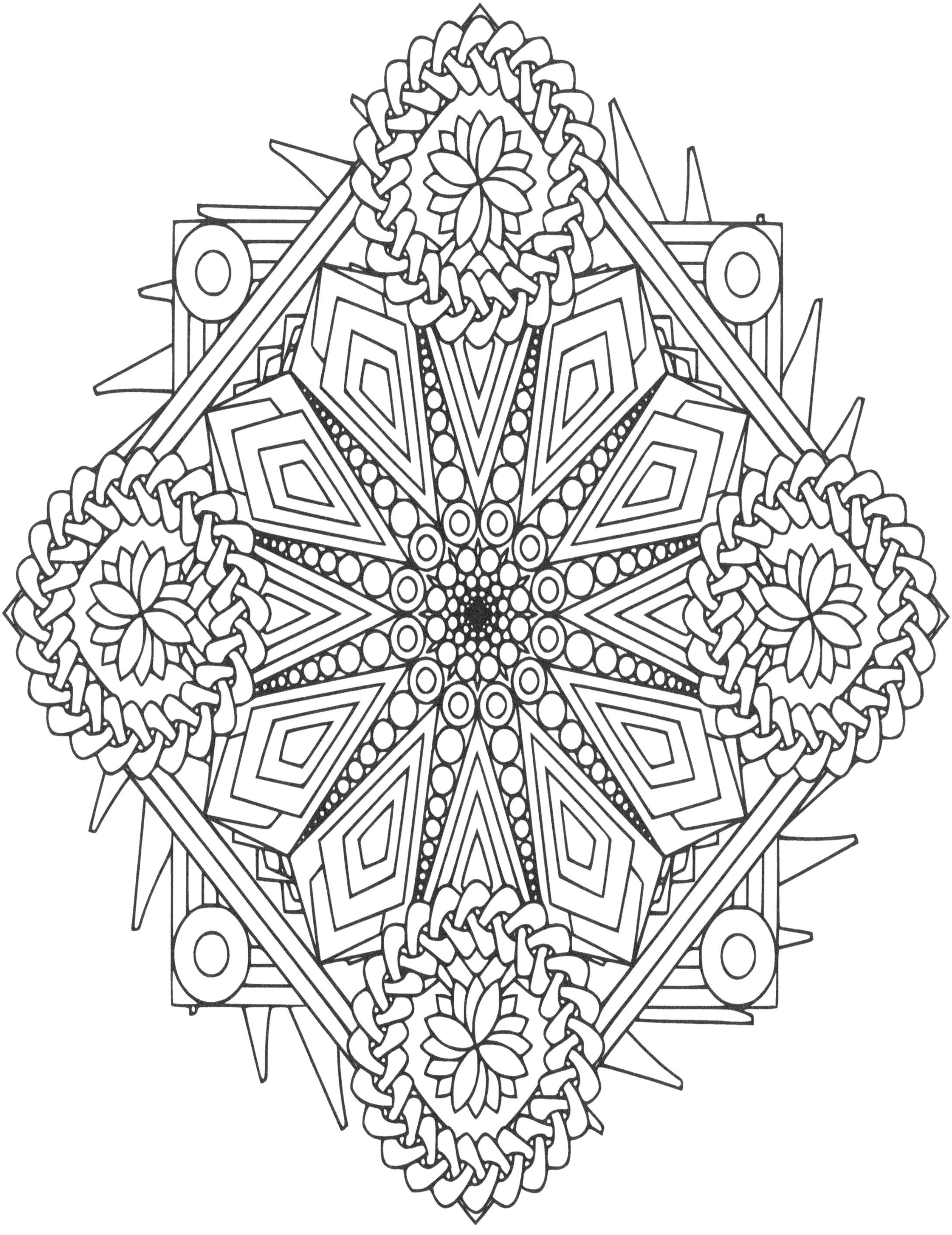

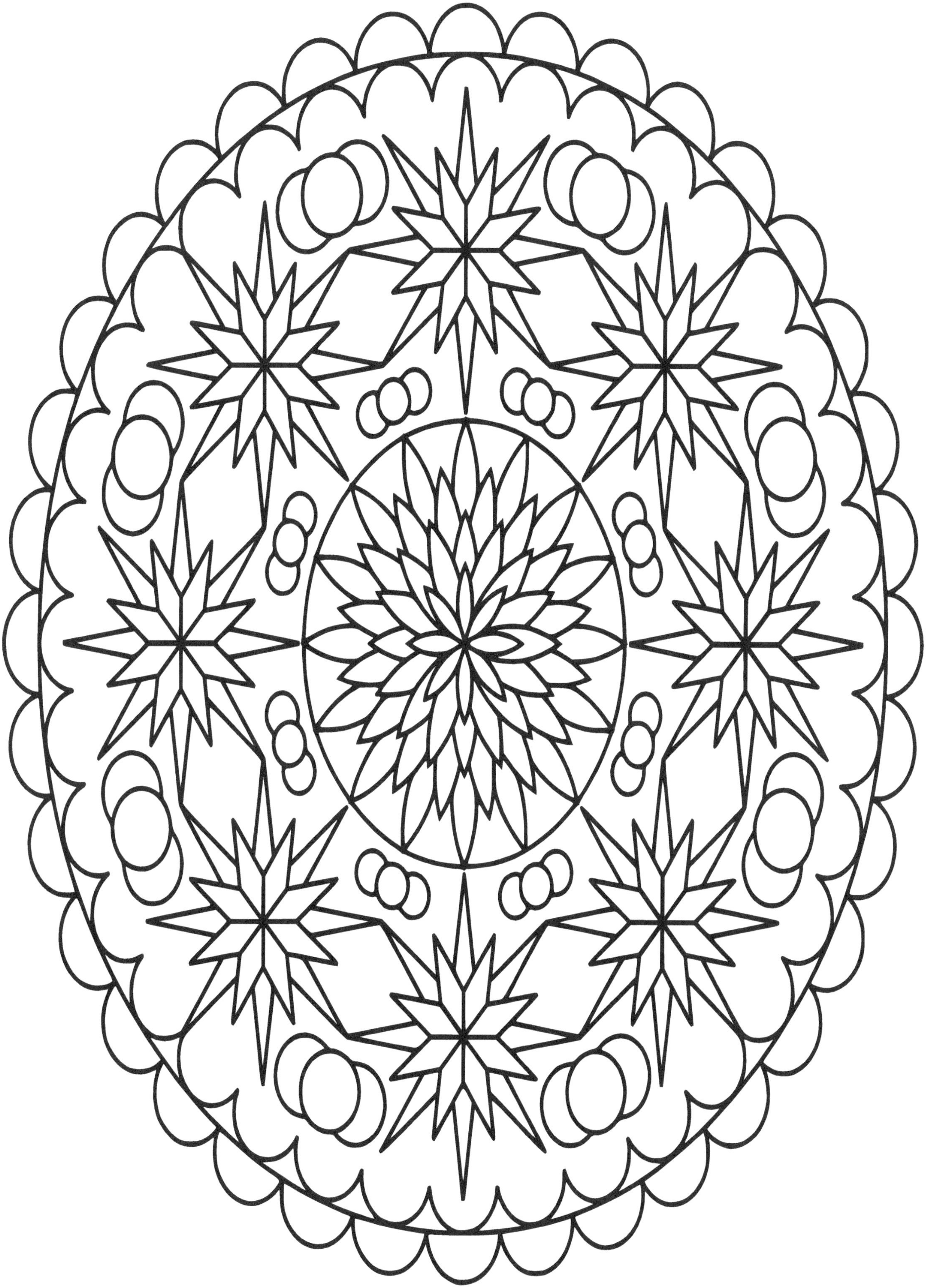

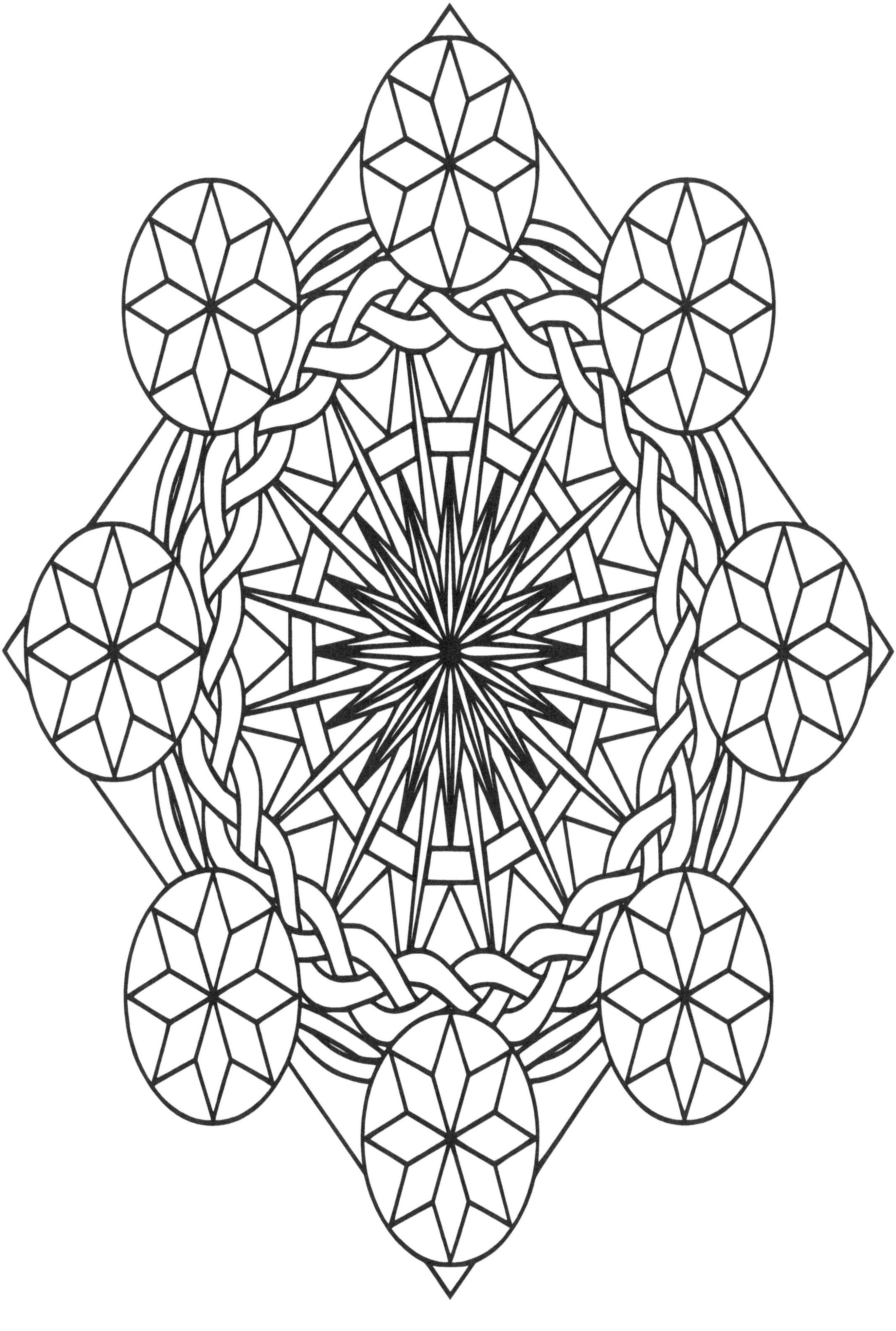

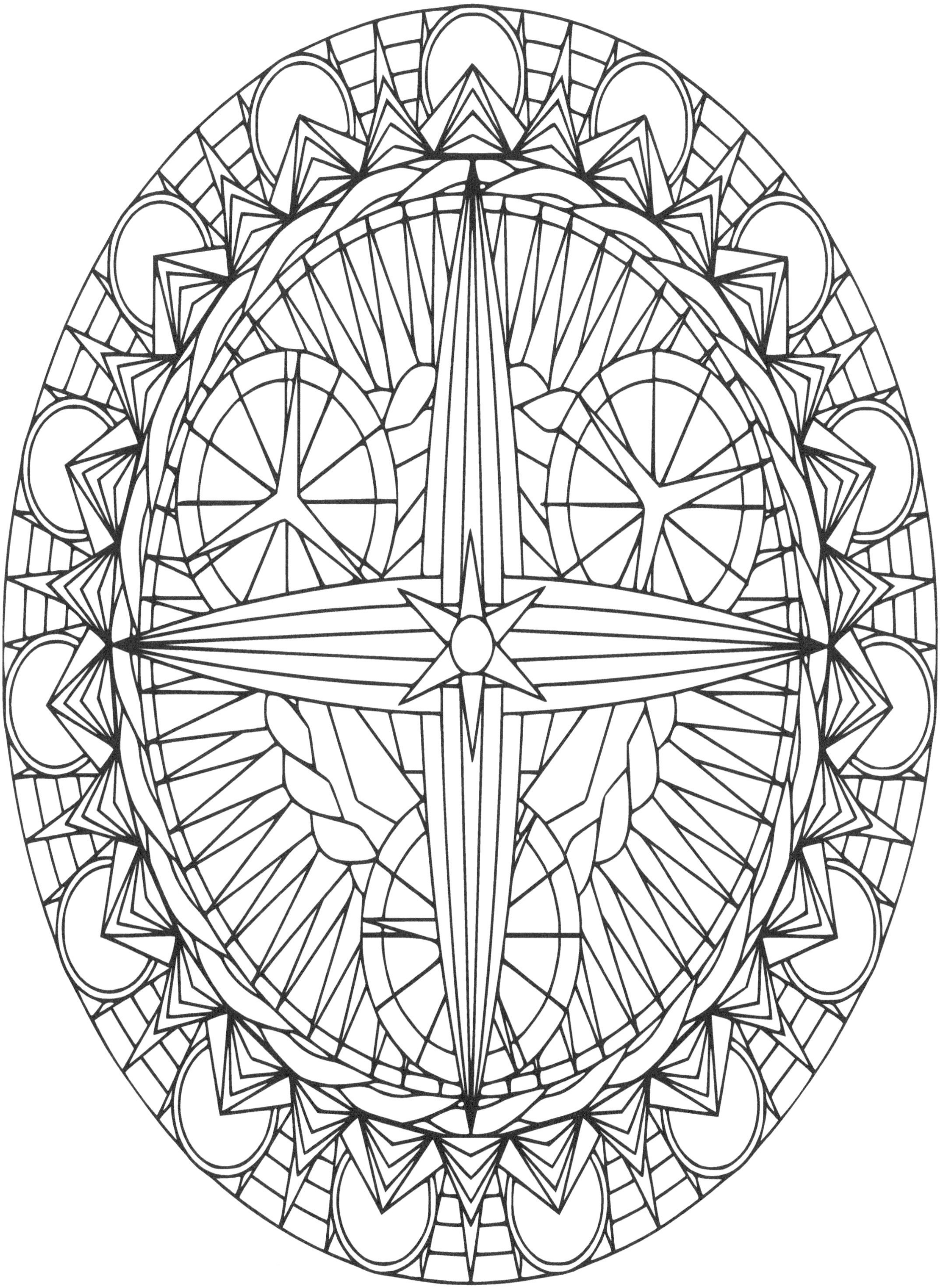

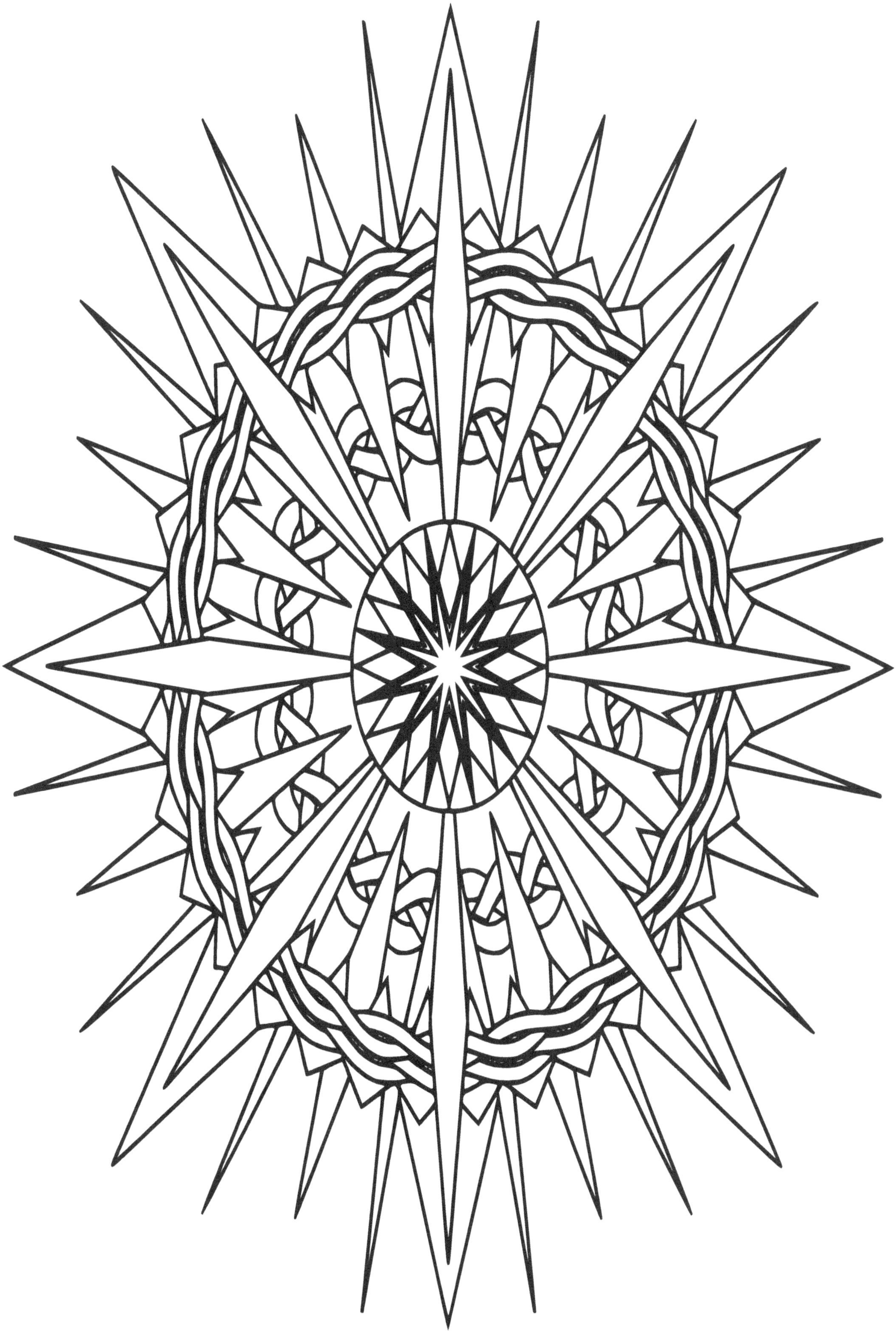

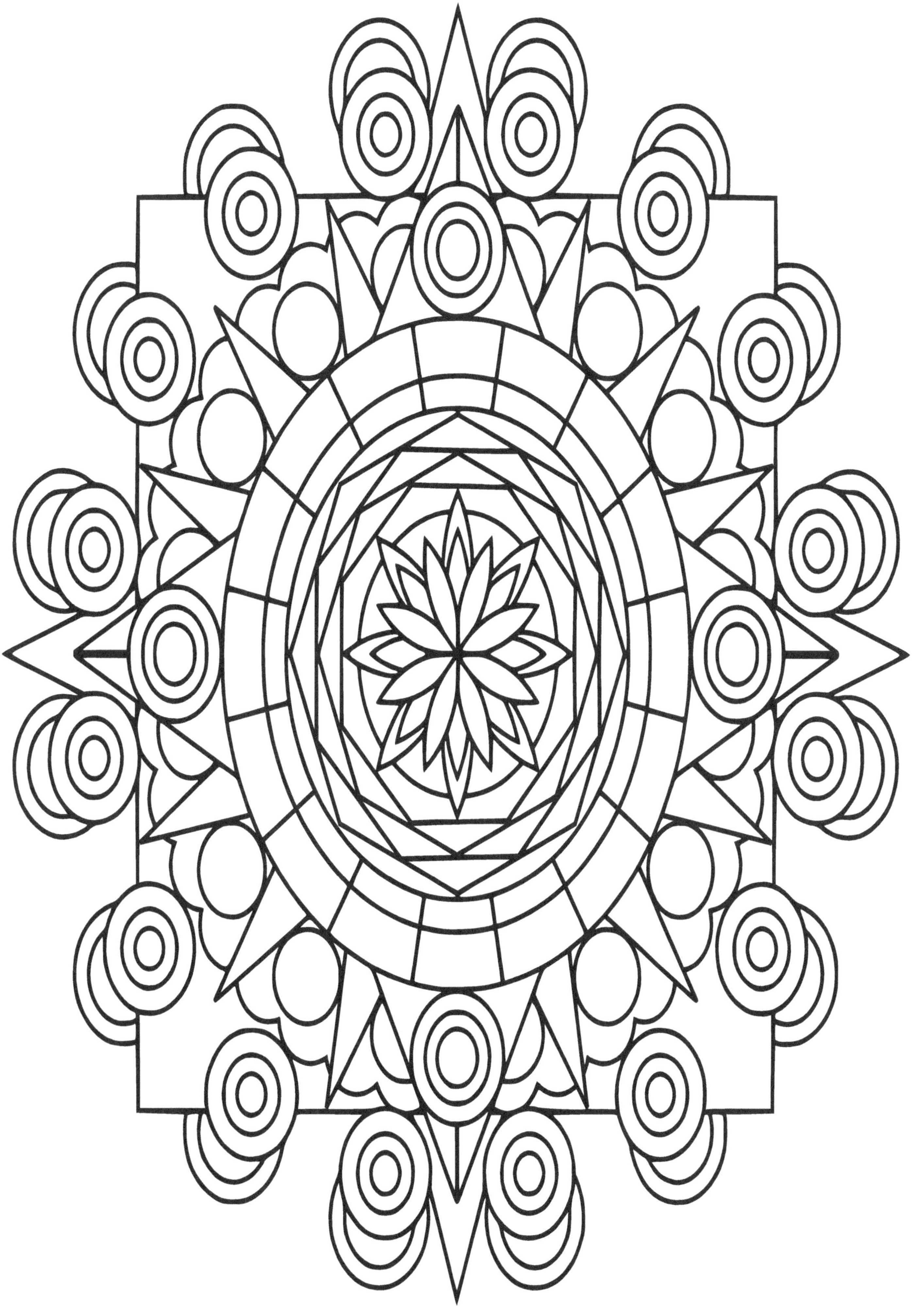

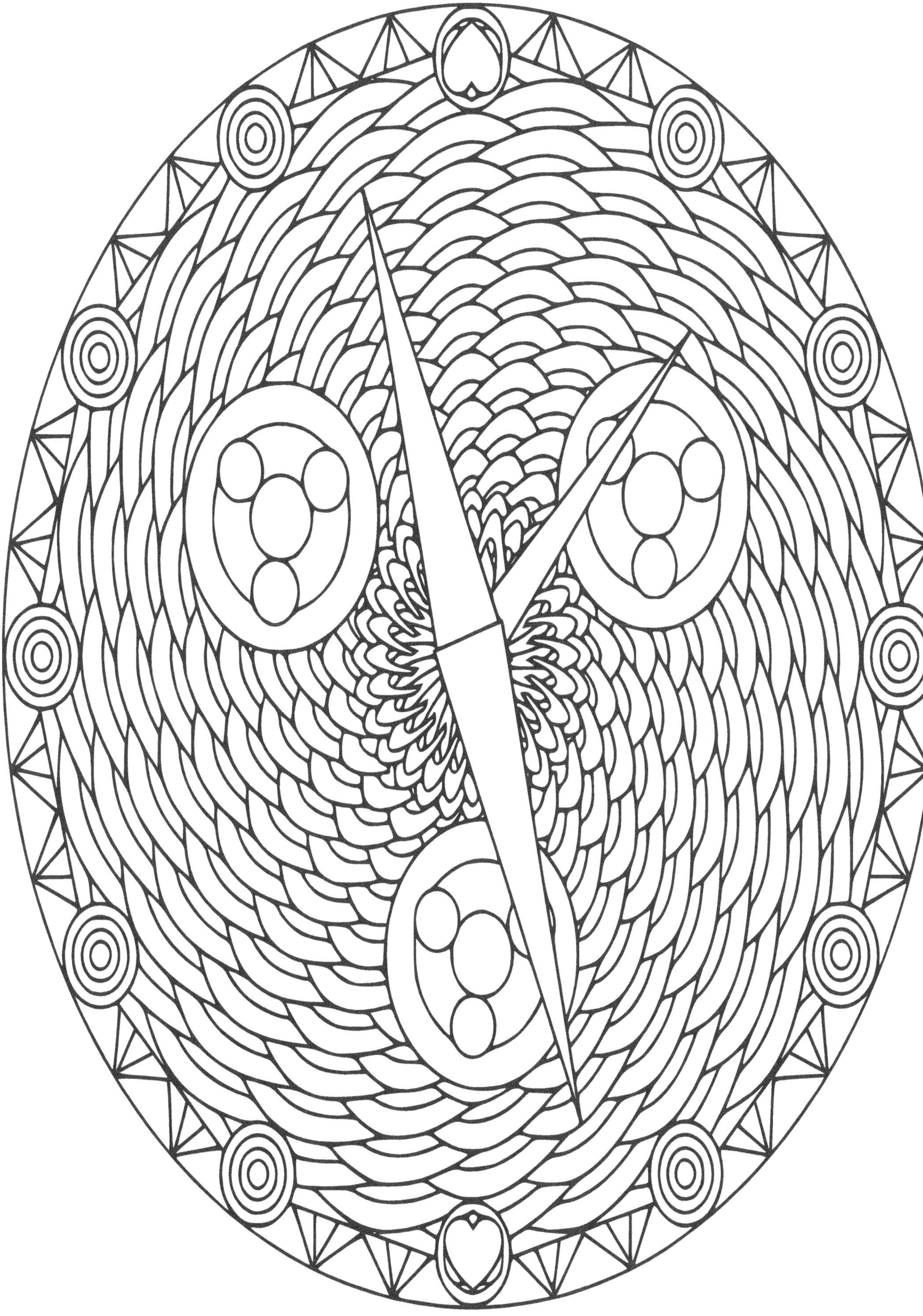

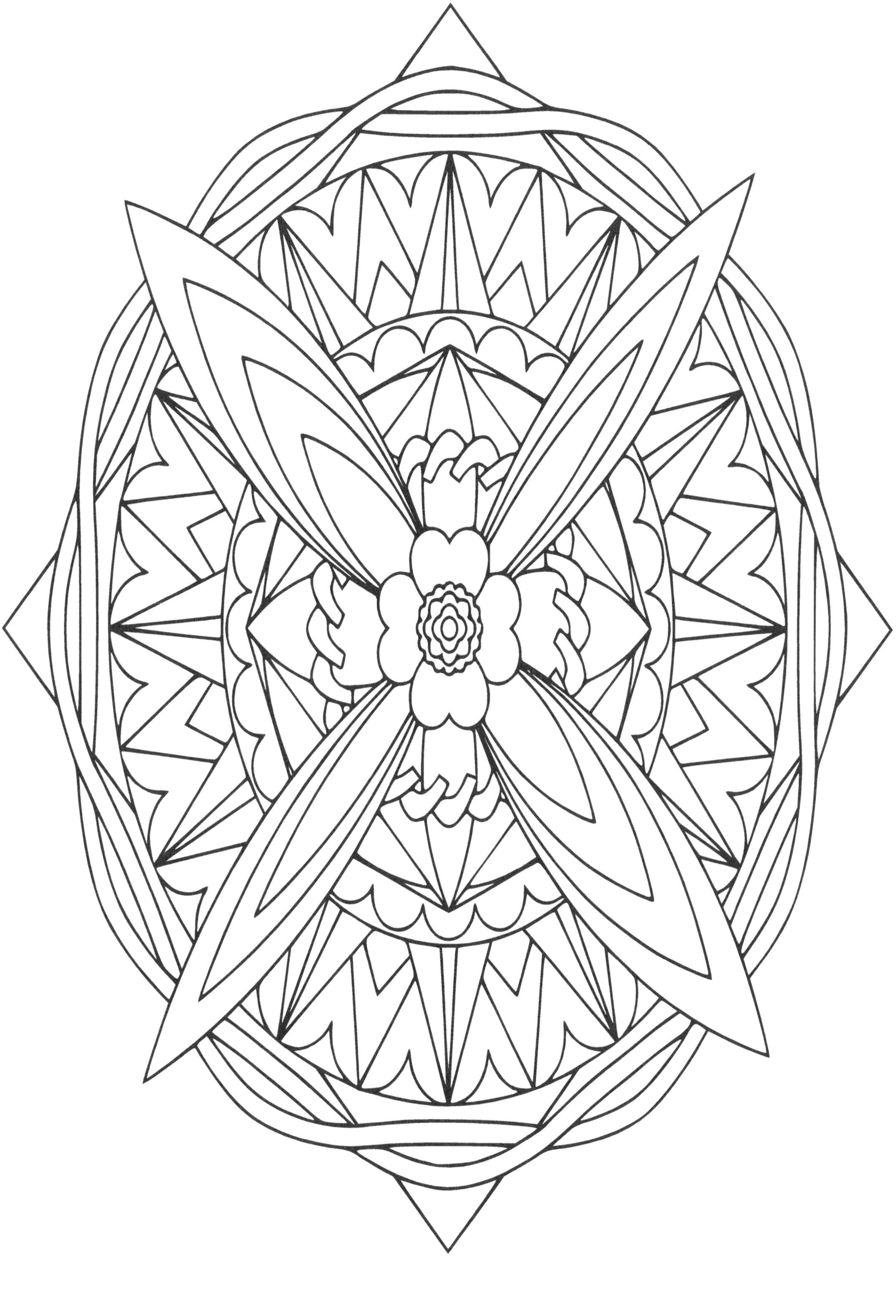

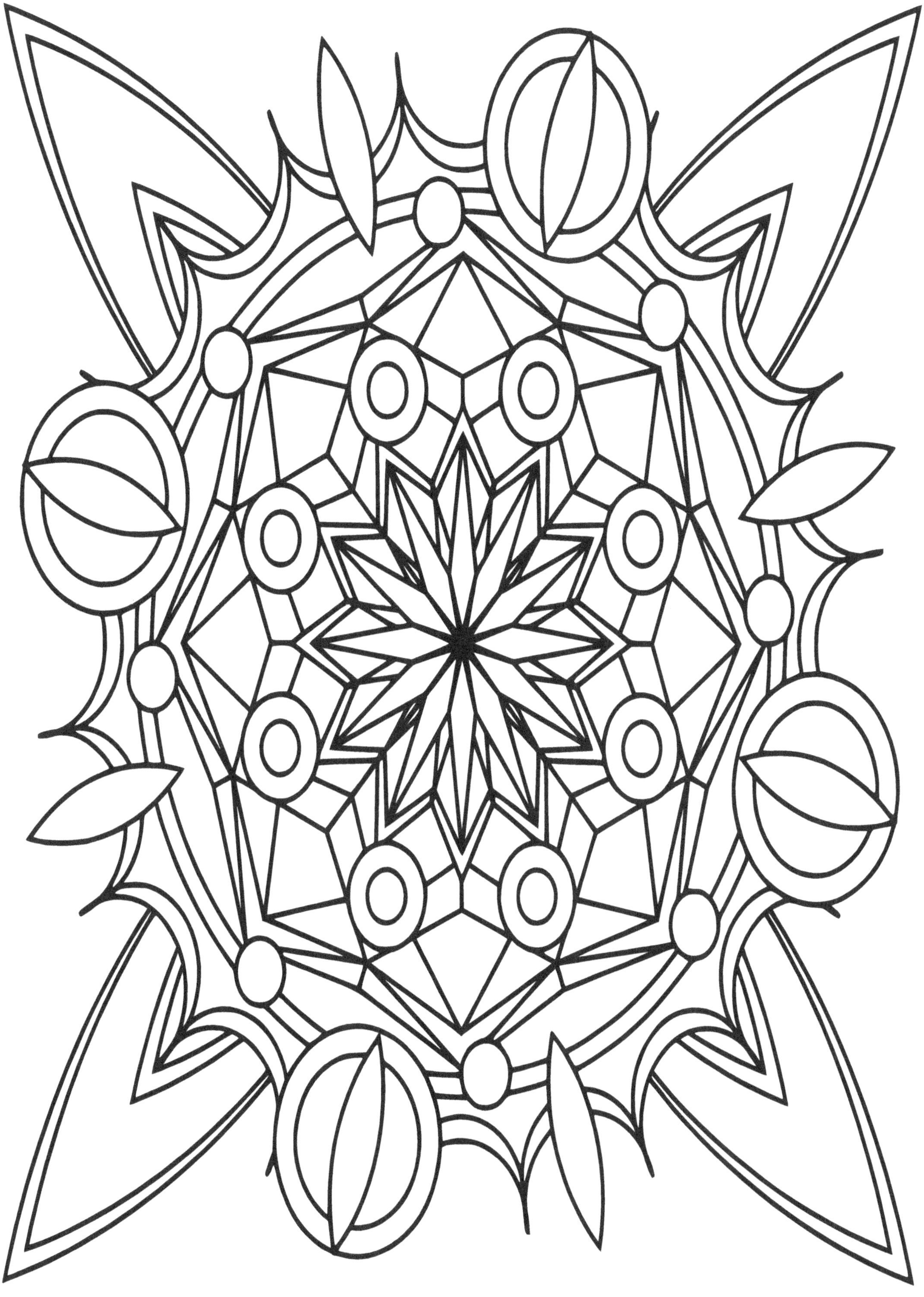

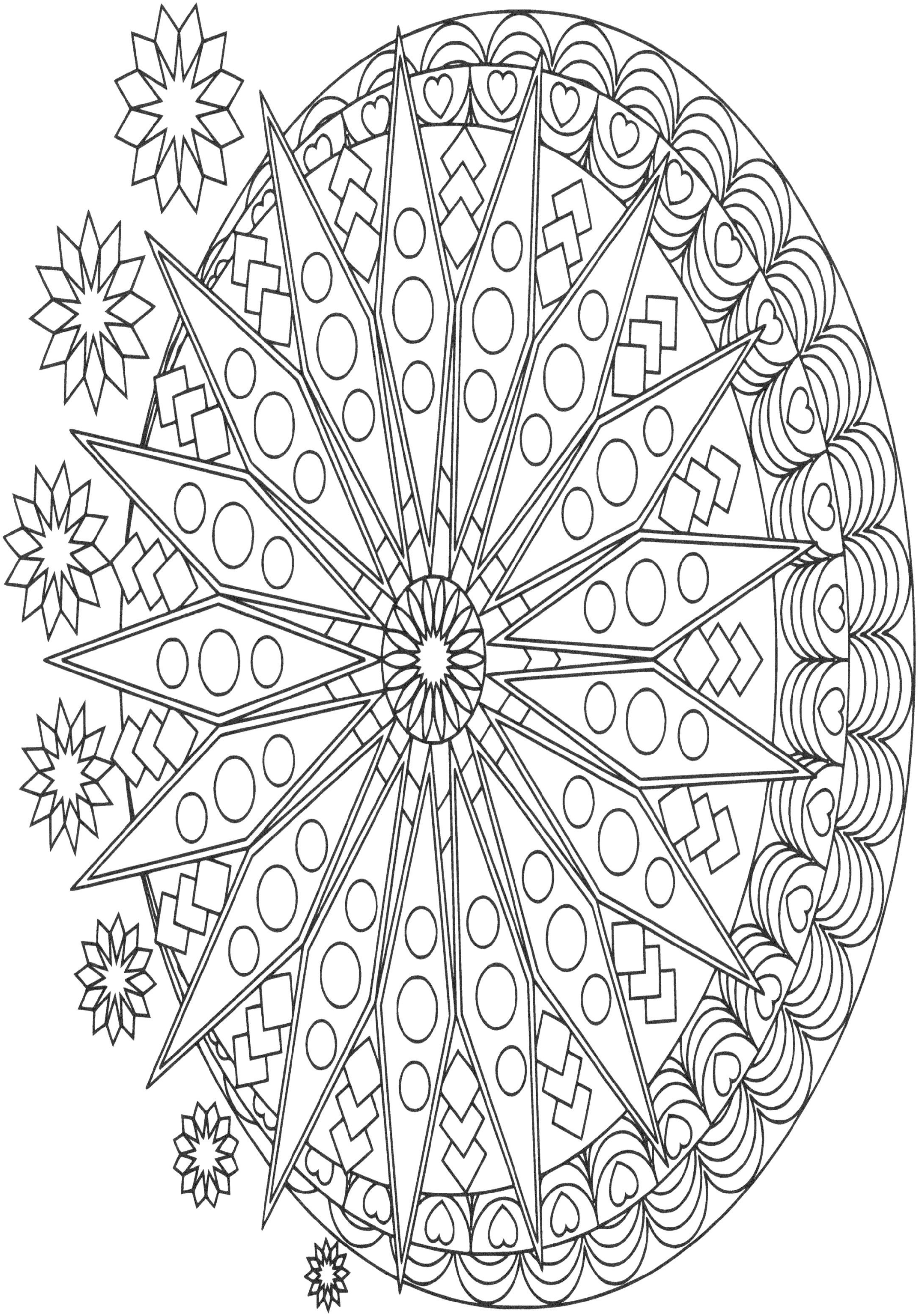

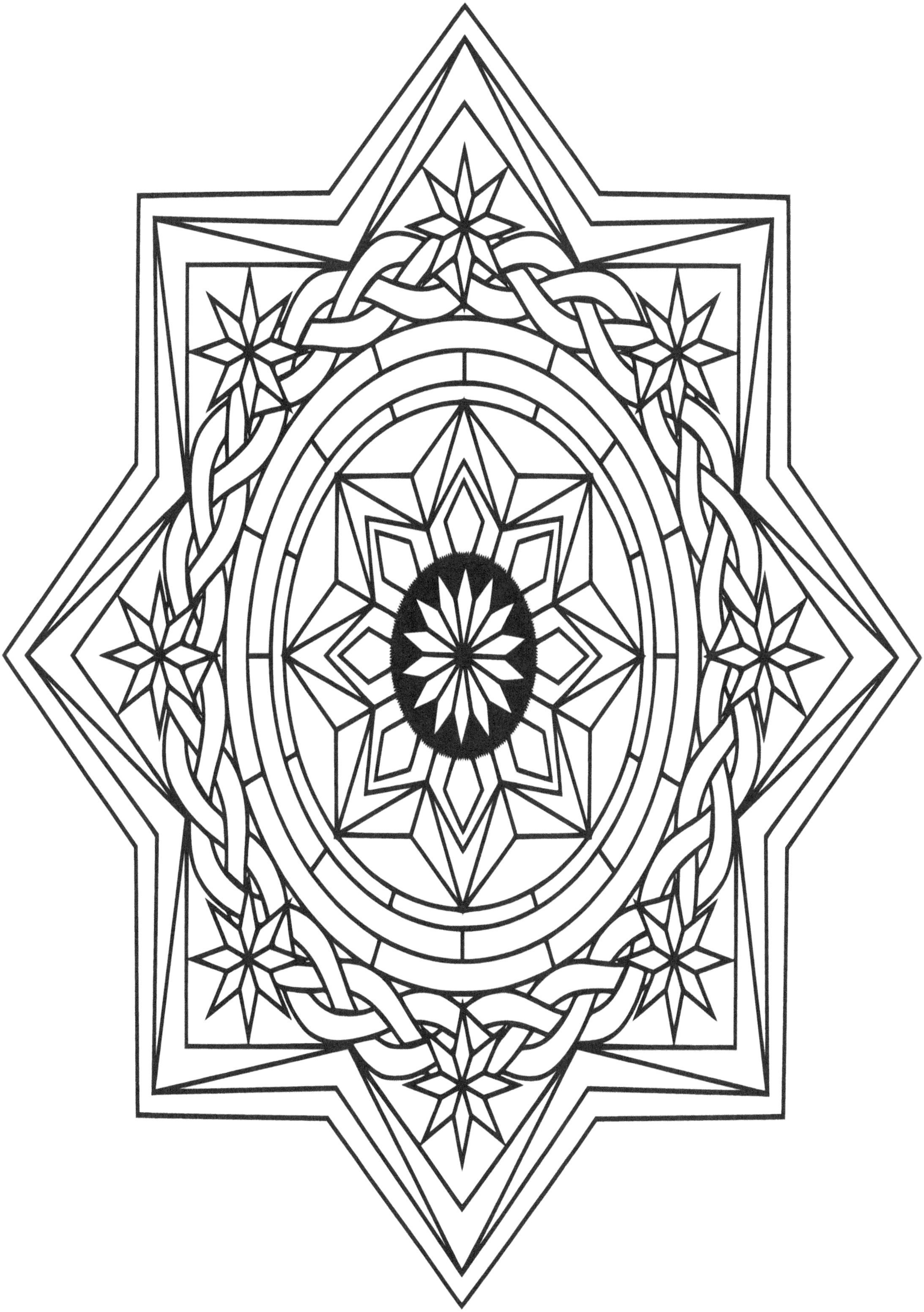

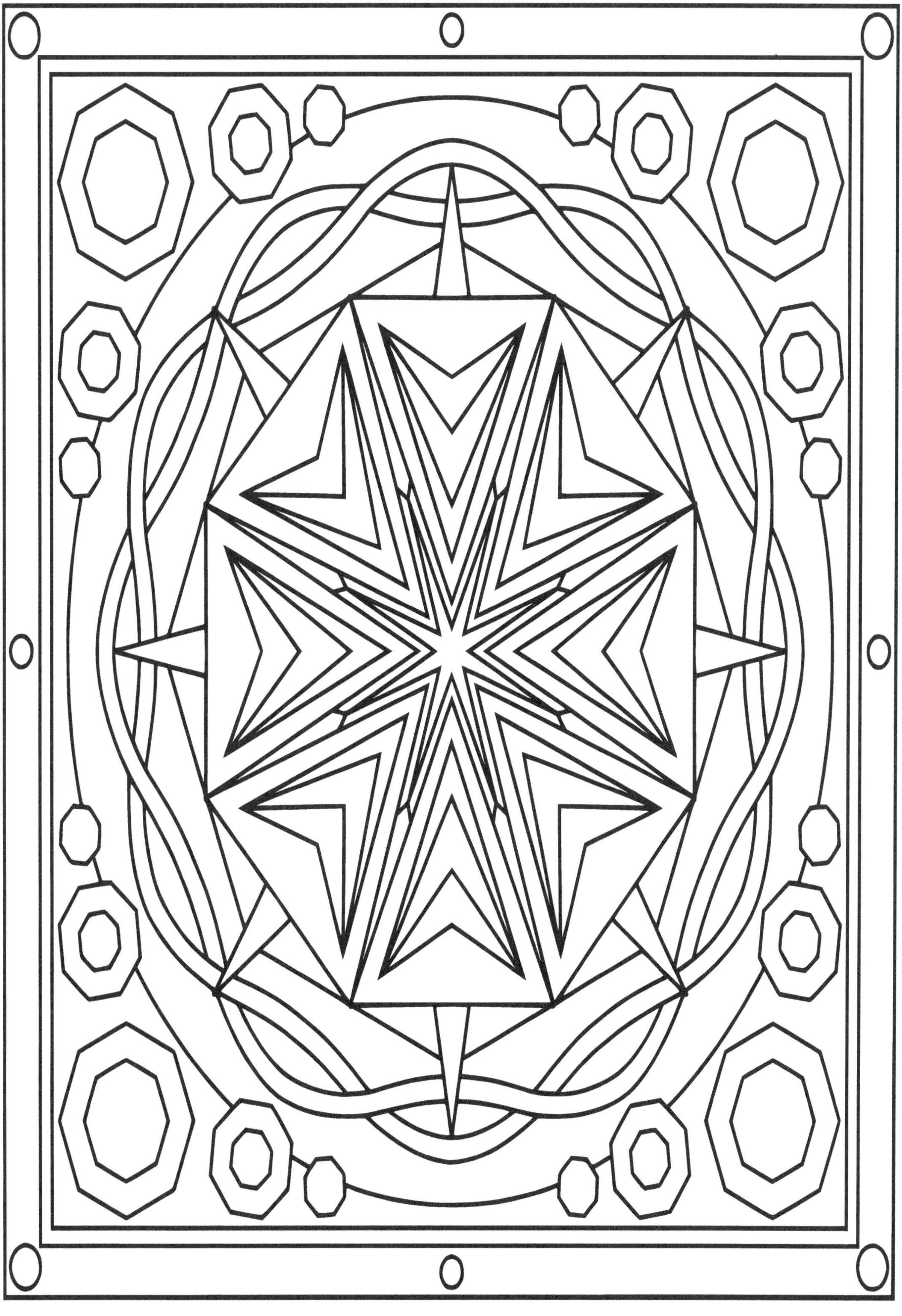

www.ingramcontent.com/pod-product-compliance
Lightning Source LLC
Chambersburg PA
CBHW081842170526
45167CB00007B/2883
* 9 7 8 1 4 9 9 3 2 8 3 6 3 *